HOW TO BE A
GOOD
MOM

HOW TO BE A GOOD MOM

STEPHEN & JANET BLY

MOODY PRESS

CHICAGO

All Scripture quotations, unless noted otherwise, are from the *New American Standard Bible*, © 1960, 1962, 1963, 1968, 1971, 1972, 1973, 1975, and 1977 by The Lockman Foundation, and are used by permission.

Library of Congress Cataloging in Publication Data

Bly, Stephen A., 1944-
    How to be a good mom / by Stephen and Janet Bly.
      p.   cm.
    Includes index.
    ISBN 0-8024-3572-6
    1. Motherhood—United States.   2. Mothers—United States—
Psychology.   3. Motherhood—Religious aspects—Christianity.
I. Bly, Janet. II. Title.
HQ759.B627   1988
306.8'743—dc19   87-31260
                                                          CIP

1 2 3 4 5 6 7 Printing/RR/Year 92 91 90 89 88

Printed in the United States of America

To Alice and Betty,
Myrtle and Frances,
Katie and Marie

Contents

1

Why Mother's Day Is Bigger Than Father's Day

I *shouldn't even be here.*

The thoughts kept pounding in my head. *I'm a busy person. It's a work day. I'm sure someone needs me at the office.*

But someone else needed me too. That someone was my five-year-old son, Aaron. The occasion was a trip to the doctor's office to treat a serious infection.

Following in the Bly tradition, Aaron hates shots. And the anticipation of what was coming loomed before him for almost an hour as we sat in the waiting room. He alternated between tears and relative calm while I fumed. *What am I doing here? This is a job for his mother.*

Finally we shuffled into an examination room, and things got serious. The whole office looked and smelled like a shot. At last the doctor entered—smiling. He examined the patient and left—smiling. "A shot of antibiotic will clear this up in no time," he chirped on the way out the door.

Aaron gasped for breath and tried to hold back the sobs. "I want my mommy!" he managed. I couldn't have agreed with him more.

After what seemed an eternity, two nurses and a huge hypodermic needle entered the room. Aaron looked for a place to hide. In between efforts to talk to him and comfort him, I kept mumbling, "Never again. This is his mother's job."

He sat quietly in the car as we headed for home. "You know, Dad," he said in his mature reasoning, "Mommy is better at this than you are."

Aha! I thought, *I knew it. This is one of the things moms are supposed to do!*

But is it? We all have our opinions of what moms should do. Society collects these ideas and sketches a vast composite of "ideal motherhood."

But what makes a good mom anyway? Doing everything exactly right? Producing good kids?

Here are some common assumptions we've gleaned from our acquaintances.

A Good Mom:
- never bakes biscuits from little cardboard tubes that go "pow!"
- appears instantly whenever any family member yells, "Mom!"
- knows exactly what garment each child wants to wear to school each day and has it washed, mended, and hung in the closet
- is *always* home when you call
- uses coupons to save a minimum of fifteen dollars on each visit to the grocery store
- raises kids who are potty trained before age two and stop sucking thumbs by kindergarten
- cherishes the idea of home schooling
- never raises her voice
- never needs to run after a school bus with a forgotten lunch pail
- never dreads teacher conferences
- attends every T-ball and soccer game in hose and heels (fresh from the office, of course, or some other world-expanding venture)
- never leaves kids with runny noses in the church nursery
- never says no to the P.T.A.
- never feeds her kids anything with white sugar, white flour, or salt
- can fix flat tires on rush hour freeways

- owns an ironing board and knows how to use it
- eats as much as Junior, but stays as slim as Sis
- keeps a regimented family schedule of daily tooth flossing and Bible memorization

We each have our composites of good moms—or poor ones—but mothers of all kinds and types still hold an honored place in our society. The four-by-twenty-foot banner across the back of the rescue mission never reads, "Have you written to your father lately?" The sign always trumpets, "Have you written to your mother?"

The number one holiday in America for restaurant business is not Father's Day. It's Mother's Day. In fact, Mother's Day boasts a flourishing bonanza for greeting card stores, florists, candy companies, and most other retailers.

But never have we heard complaints about the disparity of celebrations between these two holidays. That may be because most of us carry around the nagging realization "You haven't done enough for Mom!" We hold to the "balanced ledger" concept of relationships: if a relationship is to be strong and healthy, an equal amount of give and take is needed from both sides.

But it's a lousy theory, simply because it doesn't work. For one thing, it's too hard to keep score. For another, mothers have a head start by many years. Faced with such an impossible task, we feel that the least we can do is to send flowers or candy once a year in May.

However, moms struggle with guilt burdens of their own. They may give little thought to the "balanced ledger," but few mothers can ignore comparisons to "ideal motherhood." In the contest of ideal motherhood the emphasis is to "do everything right." If the children turn out well, she is deemed "a good mom." If they don't, she lives under the strain that somewhere, somehow, she must have "done something wrong." This prevailing theory is supported in psychology classes that pronounce, "If you're messed up in any way, it's because of faulty parental influence."

No wonder moms feel, at times, like failures. Television sounds out one image of motherhood. Women's magazines list the "four easy steps." Your kids tell you about a mother down the street, and your husband tells you that's "not the way I was raised."

Many of today's moms find themselves under the gun of unreach-able ideals. In response to the pressure, some drop out.

Laurie resides in a commune in Oregon somewhere, and Stan at-tempts to rear their daughters. Laurie told Stan she was going to Eu-gene to visit her sister, who was ill. That was nearly six years ago.

Kay never goes anywhere. But she's nearly as distant from her fam-ily as is Laurie. She drags out of bed by noon, heads for the Jack Dan-iels, flips on the soaps, and sinks into oblivion.

Maureen is the best seamstress in town. She ought to be, because she spends six to ten hours a day at her machine. She'd rather make the kids new clothes than wash the ones they have. Her irate hus-band once showed us their kitchen, where every dish in the house lay in dirty piles on the counters. The floors were caked with grime, cobwebs billowed in the ceiling corners, and Christmas decorations hung on the walls. "From two years ago," he said.

The kids hadn't bathed in a week, but they would get new shirts. Maureen overcompensated in one area to avoid the others.

Patty doesn't spend much time with home chores. Her real estate job occupies her days, evenings, and weekends. When the kids com-plain, Patty says, "Well, without this job you wouldn't have the mo-torcycle or the braces on your teeth or the big-screen television." The truth is, without that job Patty would go crazy with the responsi-bilities of being a mom.

Laurie, Kay, Maureen, Patty—in one way or another, they're all dropouts. The pressure to perform got too great, and they reached out for an alternative.

Four basic misconceptions account for most of the pressure.

THE MISCONCEPTIONS OF MOTHERHOOD

MOTHERING IS EASY

The uptown lady in the tailor-made silk suit glanced at her watch several times as she stood in the wedding reception line. With a sigh of impatience, she chatted with the young woman behind her, who was holding a baby.

"I've really got to get going. I wish they'd take the pictures after the reception, don't you?"

The woman shifted the baby to her other hip. "Well, it is kind of slow. Do you have a long drive yet today?"

"I've got a plane to catch. I've got a presentation to make for my company in New York tomorrow."

"Oh? What kind of work do you do?"

"I'm a marketing executive for a department store chain. And you? What kind of work do you do?"

The young lady took a folded diaper off her shoulder and wiped the baby's chin. "Oh, me? I don't do anything. Just raising kids, you know."

No job on earth takes more physical, mental, social, emotional, and spiritual strength than being a good wife and mother. If a woman is looking for the easy life she might try teaching tennis, cutting diamonds, or joining a roller derby team. There is nothing easy about good mothering. It can be back breaking, heart wrenching, and anxiety producing. And that's just the morning.

MOTHERING IS NATURAL

Jerry raced through the house searching for Kathy. "That was Mom on the phone. She and Dad are downtown right now. Thought they'd just stop by for a little visit. Oh, I didn't even ask them if they could stay over for lunch. Naturally, you'll want to straighten up things and pull something out of the freezer."

"Naturally?" Kathy stared. "What I'd like to do naturally is hop in the car and flee to Palm Springs—alone."

By nature, all of us are self-centered, prideful, and petty. Our nature tells us, "Let Nick make the bed for a change." "Tracy can sew up her own skirt." "Clayton can walk home from school. A little rain won't hurt him." "If Jerry's folks don't bother letting us know they are coming to town until ten minutes before they arrive, then they can live with 'thingies' on the rug and write their names in the dust on the table."

There's no innate quality in a mother that gives her delight in cleaning vomit off an antique quilt. In fact, part of the struggle to be a good mom is to overcome some natural, even sinful, inclinations. Perhaps that was a part of what God meant when He told Eve, "In pain you shall bring forth children" (Genesis 3:16).

MOTHERING IS ALWAYS FUN

A large station wagon pulled in next to us as we stopped along the interstate highway at a fast food joint. Obviously the occupants were on a vacation trip, as we were. We watched the dad climb out and unfasten a child carrier. He cradled a baby while three boisterous kids clambered out the back door. Two more banged on the rear window. The mother, wearing a maternity smock, piled out with a toddler in tow. We noticed the mother's face. She looked like someone who'd been locked in an oriental bamboo torture cage.

Let's face it, if housework was so fulfilling, if being cooped up in a house all day with little people was such sport, then why do we have such a difficult time finding anyone to take on either of these chores even for small stretches when we so desperately need a break?

Traipsing off to a dress shop with a hundred dollar bill in your purse—now that's fun. Having a candlelight dinner at that exclusive restaurant overlooking the harbor—that's sheer delight. Putting another log in the fireplace, relaxing in the recliner, and reading a novel—pure joy.

Mothering has its many pleasurable moments, but it takes a total commitment of the will to weather all the sticky times in between.

A MOTHER IS REPAID FOR ALL SHE DOES

Ruth stayed up until 2:00 A.M. to complete Shirley's cheerleading outfit because no one remembered to tell her that it had to be ready for pictures the next day. She breathed a sigh of relief as Shirley went off to school in the new outfit. Then she got a call at noon. "Mom, I've got to have the matching jacket too! Really, Mom, I'll just die if I'm the only one without a jacket."

So Ruth set aside her own plans, ran down to the yardage shop, and plunked back down into the sewing room. Years of performance under pressure came through for her, and the jacket, complete with monogrammed name, was ready for the four o'clock pictures. "Mom, can you wait to give me a ride home?" Shirley pleaded after Ruth had brought her the jacket.

Then it was time to chop the chicken meat, stir-fry some veggies, toss a salad, and call everyone to dinner. At seven o'clock Ruth groaned as she remembered the P.T.A. meeting. She longed to col-

lapse in a chair or a warm bathtub, but this was the meeting to discuss who would be in charge of the annual carnival. Last time she
missed a meeting like that, she was chosen chairman. She wasn't
about to have that happen again.

As Ruth ran a comb through her hair, smoothed on some lipstick,
and grabbed a sweater, she yelled at Shirley, "Honey, I need you to
do the dishes for me tonight."

The meeting dragged on and on because no one would volunteer
to be carnival chairman. She wasn't quite sure how it happened, but
about ten o'clock a bleary-eyed Ruth agreed to do it another year.
Back home again, she dragged herself into the kitchen. All the dishes remained exactly where she'd left them.

Oh, sure, Shirley would receive a proper reprimand in the morning, but Ruth was looking for more than obedience. Gratitude,
maybe?

Interaction with other human beings, whatever the context, will
require us to deal with disappointment and irritation. However, the
family context offers some rich additional dividends that other
groups can't provide. Here are just two of the rewards that make
mothering worthwhile.

Companionship. There is a deep human joy in being intimately involved with another person's life. We are created to be social people.
We are to communicate with others. Our ability to laugh, cry, struggle, feel, succeed, and even fail with others is an important part of
what it means to be human.

But we can't jump into just anybody's or everybody's life at that
level. We have the capacity for that level of intimacy with only a few
folks. Families provide the built-in structure for nurturing that kind
of companionship.

Kristie met her dad at the door. "Shh, Mommy's crying. It's because she lost her dolly."

"What?"

"She lost her dolly," Kristie repeated with a knowing hush.

Out in the kitchen Phyllis greeted her husband.

"What's this about crying over a lost doll?"

Phyllis grinned sheepishly. "Oh, it was one of those things that
came over me all of a sudden. Kristie and I spotted these dolls at a

store today. I hadn't seen any like them in years, though I had one when I was Kristie's age.

"Anyway, I got to telling Kristie about mine, and I remembered about our family's trip back to Ohio to see my grandmother. I took my doll into a diner and forgot it. By the time I remembered it, we were many miles away. Even so, my father turned back for it. But it wasn't there. I cried all the way to Ohio. I guess I got all torn up thinking about the lonely, deserted doll and the heartbroken little girl. Kind of silly, huh?"

Her husband looked at her strangely, but not Kristie. She understood. And now she and her mother shared a secret from the past that brought them even closer together.

Satisfaction. None of us can escape the inner drive to have meaning and purpose in life. Few of us purposely choose a shallow, insignificant existence. A tree or a butterfly doesn't worry about what impact it has left on its turf when it is gone. We would like to think we've helped this old world be a little more loving, a little more generous, a little more peaceful. At the least, we want to be a part of preserving the same quality of life that we have enjoyed.

We teach our children everything from morals to manners, not merely to keep them in line but because we're convinced those things will produce the most joy and harmony in their lives.

Gretchen listened intently to the valedictorian's speech. It was, quite possibly, the best she'd heard in her twenty years as English teacher at the high school. The attractive, poised young lady at the podium spoke clearly about the joy of accomplishment, the place of education, and the celebration of friendships. She boldly proclaimed her faith in God and her gratitude for His guidance.

Then she took a moment to give special thanks for some lessons her parents had taught her. Gretchen put her hand to her mouth and tried to hold back the tears when the speech ended with "Thanks, Mom and Dad—I love you."

As she wiped her eyes she knew it was the best graduation talk she had ever heard, even if the young lady at the podium was her daughter.

Satisfaction comes from having a lasting, positive impact on the lives of others. Few people on earth have as much potential for that kind of influence as does a mother.

Setting aside the misconceptions, and the array of varying standards, where does a woman turn to find a sane list of expectations for being a good mother?

The only consistently reliable source is the Bible. Psychology systems come and go. Advice columnists are hit and miss and require much discernment. Even friends don't always see the total picture.

Now some might complain that a woman who turns to the Bible for guidance about motherhood is just trading the narrow rules of society for the even narrower rules of religion. It's true that the Bible can be used to clobber folks into conformity, but that's not its Author's intention. The Bible itself is a rather impartial conveyor of truth. It states correct behavior and beliefs, describes incorrect behavior and beliefs, and then tells the consequences of each. You are left to choose what to do with the data.

One general outline for being a wife and mother is found in Proverbs 31. Many Christian women, familiar with the passage, will cringe at this suggestion. They view that chapter as living proof that they have failed to be the ideal wife and mother God expects them to be.

But the passage wasn't given to us to point out failure. It's meant for encouragement. Here's how.

1. It affirms some of the things that you are already doing right. And moms need all the affirmation they can get.

2. Most moms know they could try a little harder, and would like to improve, but just don't know where to begin. A passage like Proverbs 31 can give some direction. Instead of avoiding the passage, memorize it in order to provide on-the-job guidance.

Let's focus on the overall spiritual principles of the passage and set aside the cultural details of "wool and flax," "merchants," "maidens," "spindles," "vineyards," and "lighting lamps."

THE PROVERBS 31 WOMAN

IS TRUSTWORTHY (V. 10)

Reliable; to be counted on; consistent; secure; realistic. Dinner is cooked. There's a bandage on Junior's knee. The dry cleaning is picked up. And more of the same can be expected tomorrow, if needed.

Being dependable, tried and true, is not always quickly rewarded. In fact, such a trait can be taken for granted. You can check out your trustworthy factor by noticing an absence of complaints, rather than a chorus of praise.

IS VIRTUOUS (V. 11)

Morally excellent; learns from past mistakes; keeps to her principles; works to understand the difference between what's good and what's not.

"But solid food is for the mature, who because of practice have their senses trained to discern good and evil" (Hebrews 5:14).

A mother becomes virtuous not by heritage or by avoiding everything that's disagreeable but by practice—by training her heart and mind to speak against evil and welcome good.

IS INDUSTRIOUS (VV. 13, 14, 28)

Hard working; diligent; active; busy; persistent. She hangs in there with tough tasks when her body and mind tell her to quit. She sticks with a worthy project until it's done to her satisfaction. She spends her time producing things, rather than merely using up things.

IS GENEROUS (V. 15)

Unselfish; considerate; kindhearted; ungrudging; willing to give or share. If Junior finishes his dessert and wants a bite of someone else's, who does he ask first? But then, giving away a bite of pie might be a lot easier than giving away an hour.

IS WISE (vv. 16, 27)

Perceptive; intuitive; thoughtful; shrewd; uses well the knowledge she has; aims for practical, God honoring goals and uses the highest course available to achieve those goals. This may mean offering sound advice for the use of the checkbook or credit cards or storing up answers to questions that haven't been asked yet.

IS STRONG (v. 17)

Stable; sure of herself; able to withstand pressure. That could imply physical or emotional, as well as spiritual stamina. Years of proper conditioning through daily exercise, balanced diet, regular devotions, organized schedules, and mini-vacations develop strong moms.

IS COMPASSIONATE (v. 19)

Tender; sympathetic; responsive and warm; willing to offer constructive help. She listens to your hurts, even when she can see both sides of the situation. She holds in her "I told you so" or "That's the breaks, kid."

IS DIGNIFIED (v. 28)

Stands tall with grace; poised. Dignity does not depend upon the cost of her clothes, the style of her hairdo, or what she or her husband do for a living. It comes from the deep inner peace of contentment and from an understanding of who she is—and isn't—and a willingness to welcome others in the same way.

Our acquaintances say this is the trait they most admire in role models and the trait most out of their own grasp. When we ask, "Why?" they reply, "Because we know how we've blown it. How can we, in all honesty, dare to pretend we have ourselves together when we know that just this morning we screamed at the kids or left the house with jelly stuck to the table and the beds unmade?"

A mother in this common predicament can still find dignity. Not by playing a role separated from reality, but by graciously accepting the facts of her world, without undue frenzy and self-debasement. By finding forgiveness from God and her family, and giving it another try. By practice.

IS SPIRITUAL (v. 30)

Knows some things are sacred; fears God; has experienced some of the greatness of God firsthand; reverences her relationship with God above everything else.

Make a note of the qualities above that you and your family already recognize as part of your life. Thank God for His part in establishing these merits in you. Ask Him for specific help in an area that makes you wince. We all have one (or more), so you're not alone. But we're aiming for a pretty high goal: to be a good mom. We need lots of those around if we're going to heal our families and our society. Such a woman, says Proverbs 31, is:

- Indispensable—"An excellent wife, who can find? For her worth is far above jewels" (v. 10).
- Satisfied with life—"She senses that her gain is good; her lamp does not go out at night" (v. 18).
- A delight to her family—"Her children rise up and bless her; her husband also, and he praises her, saying: 'Many daughters have done nobly, but you excel them all' " (vv. 28-29).

Knowing you're indispensable, being satisfied with life, finding out you are a delight to your family—sounds great, doesn't it? It should. That's the exact definition of a good mom.

2

I'm Going to Tell Mother on You

Thirteen years is a long span between children. We ought to know. Our oldest son, Russ, was sixteen and his brother Mike was thirteen when little Aaron entered the Bly family. One day we figured out the awesome facts: we'd be raising children for nearly forty years!

The good news is: we're much older, wiser, and more "spiritual" now. Aaron will be the recipient of all our accumulated wisdom. However, though that's a definite advantage, it doesn't relieve all the problems. For one thing, he's nothing like his older brothers. So we start all over there.

And it hasn't eliminated some of the old headaches, such as sibling rivalry. When Mike was seventeen and Aaron four, big brother Russell married and moved out of the house. With so little in common between the two left we anticipated a peaceful home, free from the annoying, petty frictions the two elder brothers had faced. It would be like raising two only children. Right? Wrong.

"I did not!"

"You did too."

"I did not!"

"You did too!"

"I did not!"

"I'm going to tell Mother on you!"

The quarrels sounded pretty much the same, although they were not as frequent because of the boys' different schedules. And the same judge was called upon for arbitration: dear old Mom. In our house that's the wisest move. Dad's the final word on the matter, but if you run to him right away, there's not much room for discussion. With Mom—well, Mom has been known to figure out solutions where everyone wins, victim and guilty party alike.

Most often it's by default that Mother wins the arbitrator role. She's usually the one who's there most of the time. But it's not by chance that she has the wisdom to find an equitable solution. That comes with prayer, practice, and study.

Mothers reign as defenders of kids' rights in a world where big people rule. And kids have rights. Every kid deserves certain things in this world, and moms play an important part in seeing that kids get what they deserve.

EVERY CHILD DESERVES TO KNOW

THAT GOD IS REAL AND PERSONAL

Paul said we are to turn "to God from idols to serve a living and true God" (1 Thessalonians 1:9).

God is alive, and He is true.

Now there's nothing wrong with cultivating in our children an active and creative imagination. Imagination is the sharpening of mental facilities, a function that elevates the dullest human far above the most sophisticated computer. In promoting imagination we sometimes talk of imaginary people and friends. The stuffed animals develop personalities, bogeymen hide behind doors and trees, cartoon characters come alive at amusement parks, and, of course, there are the Easter Bunny and Santa Claus.

None of the above are necessarily harmful, unless they are portrayed in terms that cause children to believe they're real beings. But we cannot allow confusion between imagination and reality in their minds. When we do that we set them up for disappointments and loss of faith in the truth. We force them to determine on their own what is real and what is imaginary. When that happens the Lord

God Almighty can be thrown out with the tooth fairy and Cookie Monster.

They need to know, right from the beginning, that God is authentic and genuine—in a category apart from fairy tales.

When they ask, "But, why don't I see Him?" we can point to a material world that provides many examples of things that exist yet aren't seen.

When our older boys were small we camped at Bowman Lake in Glacier National Park, high up in the Rockies near the Canadian border. It happens to be one of the few places left in our country where the majestic grizzly bear still roams. As we hiked down the trail around the lake we noticed a sign.

"Warning: Grizzly Bear territory. Hikers should never hike alone. Always sing or wear bells on your shoes to sound a warning. When given advance notice, most bears will flee."

Since we didn't have any bells, we began to sing. That must have worked, because we didn't see any bears. Yet we knew that grizzly bears roamed that area. When we crossed a small creek Steve hollered to the boys, "Look! Tracks!" We stared in awe at the evidence.

We returned to camp knowing that we had hiked in grizzly bear country, because we had seen the tracks left behind.

The same is true of our knowledge of God. This side of the Lord's return no person has, or will, actually see God in a literal sense.

"No man has seen God at any time; the only begotten God, who is in the bosom of the Father, He has explained Him" (John 1:18).

But anyone can learn to spot His tracks. You can see them in the harmony and beauty of creation. You can see them in the mysteries and power of creation beyond man's scope. You can see them in the truth that keeps proving itself, age after age, in the Book He left behind. You can see them in the historical, flesh and blood Jesus. You can see them in the changed lives of His followers. You can see them in your own heart, when you open it up to Him. God is alive!

They have a right to know.

In addition, God is personal.

Out in space, somewhere, we're told a planet named Uranus spins on its axis every ten hours and fifty minutes. We read that it's the seventh planet from the sun and that five moons encircle it. We've never actually seen the planet or its moons, but if we held the right telescope, and the right satellite photos, we could detect this pale, greenish disk.

No doubt about it, that would be a thrilling sight. But if a car runs over a child's pet, or a beloved relative dies, he or she definitely wants to talk to something more personal than a moon of Uranus. God is not a distant, obscure object who dwells so far above us that our actions appear insignificant. God is personal.

God knows our names. He knows what we like and dislike. He understands our inner beings. Not only that, He enjoys our friendship. We can talk to Him about anything.

God is alive, and He is personal. Every kid has a right to know that.

THAT HE'S BEEN SPECIALLY HANDMADE BY GOD

It is not by chance, but by plan, that our children look as they do. We're not plunked out on an assembly line; rather, we're fashioned at the bench of a highly skilled Craftsman.

"For thou didst form my inward parts; Thou didst weave me in my mother's womb" (Psalm 139:13).

That means that not one part of your child is a mistake. God never used inferior materials, never got in a hurry, never did a sloppy job. Not only that, but in His eyes each person turned out perfect.

A new mother shows off her baby at a grocery store. After she leaves the lady at the counter may think, *Poor thing. That was about the ugliest baby I ever saw.*

Beauty, or lack of it, depends upon who we're trying to please. The mother saw nothing but perfection in her little one. The clerk, basing her view on contemporary standards of baby beauty, ruled otherwise. Yet the mother cherished and loved the child. What more could anyone want?

The comparison with our heavenly Father is even more dramatic. Here is God, holding all power to create. He could have made you blonde, black, or purple. He could have created you six feet tall, or six inches tall. He could have formed a small nose, a large nose, no nose, or six noses. When He completed you in the image of Himself,

He didn't shake His head and start all over. Instead, He stood back, took a good look, and exclaimed, "Perfect!"

The famous singer Barbra Streisand is noted for her rather prominent, slightly crooked nose. She tells that early in her career she sought a doctor to improve her looks through plastic surgery. He agreed that the transformation could take place but also cautioned, "It is probably your nose that gives your singing voice such distinction. If I alter it, your voice may be affected."

Barbra decided to keep her nose.

A child may fail to accept himself because he doesn't measure up to his society's image of perfection. In our own society that image is mainly manufactured by a relentless, trendy media aimed at selling products. The charming ladies who graced the calendars one hundred years ago under the banner "ideal womanhood" would now be called fat. Times change. Fashions change. But God's idea of perfection doesn't.

Every child has a right to know that God found pleasure in the way He created him. God assigned specific traits to him to insure that he would best accomplish his God-given purpose.

WHAT LOVE LOOKS LIKE IN ACTION

The eleven-year-old girl hopped across the church courtyard and plopped down on a bench next to Steve. "Stacy, how's your father doing?" Steve asked. He knew her father's prolonged ill health greatly concerned them all.

Stacy shrugged. "Oh, about the same, I guess." Then she leaned closer and whispered, "You know, Mom and Dad got in a big argument last night. He was complaining about always being sick. I heard him tell my mom that she ought to leave him and find somebody who could make her happy."

With some trepidation, Steve prodded after a moment's silence. "What did she say?"

"Oh, she just told him there was no way in the world she would ever leave him, so he might as well stop talking about it."

Relieved at the answer, Steve added, "Well, Stacy, what do you think of that?"

"Oh, you know." She brightened. "That's just the way love is."

Stacy was right. And she learned that lesson the best way of all —right at home.

"So husbands ought also to love their own wives as their own bodies. He who loves his own wife loves himself; for no one ever hated his own flesh, but nourishes and cherishes it, just as Christ also does the church" (Ephesians 5:28-29).

Children need to see a love that gives without expecting anything in return. They need to experience a love that never gives up, no matter how difficult the situation. They need to observe love that allows others to proceed at their own pace, without bitterness and impatience.

They need to learn that love is (1) a physical expression, (2) a mental decision, and (3) a spiritual commitment. They need to ponder, by example, a love that rejoices when others succeed and cries when others fail. They need to relax in a love that always believes the best about the one who is loved.

All these ideas are merely theories in a book (a very good book, mind you: 1 Corinthians 13), until children see them in action.

If the statistics are right, more than half of the mothers of this country must teach these truths to their children without a father in the house. If that's your case, we urge you to consistently expose your children to a strong marriage relationship in which husband and wife openly show each other love and affection. It could be through grandparents, neighbors down the street, or a family in the church. Your children need to see love as well as hear about it.

The child psychologists of our day back up these statements. A recent article in *Parade* magazine, "Does Love Really Make the World Go Round?" concluded, "We don't love instinctively. . . . love develops in children only if they have loving family experiences, and that adult love evolves out of childhood love."

THAT IN THE WORLD THERE ARE HARD TIMES,
BUT JESUS HAS OVERCOME THE WORLD

We'd all like to shield and protect our children. We don't want them to skin their knees, catch the chicken pox, be chosen last for the baseball team, or forget their lines during the play. But we don't have the power to prevent most of those things. They are little people out in a crowded, temperamental world—a world that sometimes doesn't treat them too kindly.

Our Russ stood at the plate during the baseball playoffs. If he got a hit he would win the award for best batting average on the team. We wanted him to win. Even more, we didn't want him to lose. *He doesn't need any more disappointments this year,* we silently prayed. *Just this one time, Lord. Help him get a hit—even a bloop hit.*

But he grounded out to the second baseman. The award would go to someone else. Russ turned away from the stands where we sat. We knew he was hurting. So were we. But that's the way some breaks come.

Mike stormed home from school one day to complain that everyone called him "preacher-boy."

Steve was indignant. "Well, I'll go and talk to your teacher."

"Won't do any good." Mike moaned. "The teacher's the one who gave me the name."

We considered asking for a change of classes for Mike, but that would not guarantee that the name calling would stop. In this world there are tough times.

Aaron bolted into the house and slammed his bedroom door. Janet followed him, ready with her lecture on door slamming. But the lecture stuck in her throat when she noticed his heaving sobs.

She gently turned him over. "What happened?"

"All the kids are having a party at Billy's house, and they told me I couldn't come," he cried.

There are tough times even for four-year-olds.

Jesus warned that it would be that way. "These things I have spoken to you, that in Me you may have peace. In the world you have tribulation, but take courage; I have overcome the world" (John 16:33).

We are not offered a way out of the world until the Lord personally calls us home. But we are offered help in getting through the world. Many humans on our planet live outside a relationship with God. They are isolated, frightened, self-centered, insensitive, or insecure. From that base, man's inner nature can cause incredible hav-oc for all those around him.

Your kids deserve to know that Jesus is always on their side, always willing to help, always right there with them.

God doesn't always shield them from difficulties, but with His help they can find a way to survive, endure, and even conquer.

THAT THE BIBLE IS COMPLETELY RELIABLE

Kids live in a rapidly changing world. Not only do *they* change as they grow from one stage to the next, but everything around them is in transition. What are the hairstyles now? Which clothes are in? Which rock group is most popular?

Philosophical ideals modify. Science textbooks update. Public morals alter. Friends move. Parents split. Finances fail.

Parents, too, can be rudely shaken by the sudden changes. The contrasts between what our older boys faced and what our younger son encounters often startle us. Words so vile they once hid in murky corners of public toilets now bounce around on T-shirts. Big news about a classmate would once have been "She's adopted!" Confusion about divorce might have brought the question, "How come Billy's dad can only see him on weekends?"

Now we're likely to hear, "Her father kidnapped her when she was three. Now she's back with her mom." And terms like *clone, sperm donor, surrogate mother,* and *test tube baby* are creeping into the vocabulary.

Is there anything that remains a constant for your child's shifting environment?

The Bible does.

"All scripture is inspired by God and profitable for teaching, for reproof, for correction, for training in righteousness" (2 Timothy 3:16).

From the time they read their first words, they need to know that the Bible is unique. Everything else they ever read, study, or hear can be measured for reliability according to how closely it adheres to this one Book.

THAT LIFE WITH JESUS IS EXCITING AND ADVENTURESOME

Some kids don't want to read Bible stories, go to Sunday school, or talk about "spiritual stuff" because it's "too boring." Are they ever misinformed.

Jesus said, "I came that they might have life, and might have it abundantly" (John 10:10).

The apostles who traveled close to Jesus were, at times, threatened, starved, scared, startled, high on joy, or totally astonished. It's never boring to get close to Jesus.

Where Jesus walks the blind see, the lame leap, the deaf hear. Derelicts sober up; gang members preach; the shy speak out; the simple spout wisdom; misers shell out; and cowards stand tall.

Because Jesus has no limits, anything is possible. Loaves and fish multiply; storms still. The money for piano lessons appears out of nowhere; the mean kid down the street apologizes or moves to Buffalo; Daddy goes to church; the fever subsides.

Because God is headed somewhere, everything He does has a purpose. It's the purposeless acts that get boring. Every child should know that he or she can find his place in God's plan and be a part of "hastening the coming day of God" (2 Peter 3:12).

Human error, not divine malfunction, causes boredom. The easiest way for a kid to learn about an exciting spiritual life is to see a demonstration in his parents' life-style.

THAT OBEDIENCE TO GOD IS THE SECRET TO A FULFILLED LIFE

"If you abide in My word, then you are truly disciples of Mine; and you shall know the truth, and the truth shall make you free" (John 8:31-32).

We explain obedience to God in one of several ways.

Obey God, or He will clobber you. This is crude and not too effective, as children will soon discover that lightning doesn't usually strike immediately. Besides, this tactic puts the blame on God for all sorts of unrelated catastrophes.

It's true; disobedience generates consequences. Whoever, young or old, willfully rebels against God, stirs to action certain laws of this universe. No arguments, arrogance, or ignorance can deter the ultimate outcome. But there are better motivations for obedience.

Obey God, and He will help you achieve what you've inwardly desired all along. Jesus promised freedom. We can spend a lot of energy and resources and time trying to be free, but the Bible says freedom comes only through obedience. And we learn obedience only by giving constant attention to His Manual.

Obey God because it pleases Him. We are debtor people. We owe God something, and we can never repay Him. He sent His only Son to die for us so that we could be released from our hopeless, vicious cycle of destruction and death. His extraordinary display of love should tug at us to love Him back.

How can we properly do that?

"If you keep My commandments, you will abide in My love; just as I have kept My Father's commandments, and abide in His love" (John 15:10).

Obedience pleases Him.

Friendship with God means always growing, always gaining insights, finding a new joy in living whatever the particular circumstances.

Jesus said, "I am the bread of life; he who comes to Me shall not hunger, and he who believes in Me shall never thirst" (John 6:35).

That's a glimpse of a fulfilled life, one that cheerfully follows orders from above.

ABOUT THE THOROUGHNESS OF GOD'S FORGIVENESS

"I am writing to you, little children, because your sins are forgiven you for His name's sake" (1 John 2:12).

When the Lord forgives, He doesn't bring the matter up to us again. He doesn't bring it to others, either. He doesn't even sit around thinking about what we did. When He forgives, He is able to treat us as though we had never done the act in the first place.

We might have a difficult time discerning whether forgiveness was genuinely sought, but He never has trouble. The sincere heart always finds His arms open.

How do you teach your children about forgiveness? The same way you teach them other things. For instance, if you want them to know what a buffalo looks like, you point to a picture in a book, then watch for an opportunity to show them a live or stuffed one.

David committed adultery with Bathsheba. He repented, and God forgave.

Jonah ran away from God's will. He had a change of heart, and God forgave.

Peter denied that he knew Christ. He was overcome with sincere remorse, and God forgave.

On and on the accounts go. God constantly forgives. You show them that by examples in the Book. Then you look for a chance to see a firsthand example.

Start by forgiving your children yourself. Junior backs the new car into the mailbox. With real panic he reports it to you.

How do you forgive? By saying, "I forgive you," *and* by never bringing the matter up to him, his friends, or your friends, and allowing him to use the car the next Friday night.

Of course, there's still the matter of the dented mailbox and bashed fender. Even with God's forgiveness, there's an aftermath that can't be undone without restitution.

THAT LIFE IS JUST A PREP SCHOOL FOR ETERNITY WITH GOD

From their first encounter with death, they should understand that life goes on beyond the grave.

"In My Father's house are many dwelling places; if it were not so, I would have told you; for I go to prepare a place for you. And if I go and prepare a place for you, I will come again, and receive you to Myself; that where I am, there you may be also" (John 14:2-3).

Some day things get better. Some day everything makes sense. Some day the wicked are punished and the righteous rewarded.

Meanwhile, we're in school. God wants to teach us how to get along with each other here on earth before we're promoted to heaven.

John D. Rockefeller once said, "I will pay more for the ability to deal with people, than any other ability under the sun."

THAT GOD HEARS HIS EVERY PRAYER

"Pray without ceasing," Paul challenges in 1 Thessalonians 5:17.

Kids can never pray too much. And God speaks their language. He understands their hearts. He cares about their problems and their joys. He is anxious to act with their best interests in mind.

They can pray at night, in the morning, at mealtimes, when they need help, and when they're having fun. Introduce God as a close companion who is always available.

We cannot, though we'd like to, insure that our children will become faithful followers of Christ. Each individual child must choose for himself. But we can staunchly defend their rights.

Mom is often the highest court of appeal within the family structure. As in any other court, she must establish a set of mandates from which to make her rulings. How can you make sure your decisions will be most fair? By insisting that your children get, from God's point of view, what they deserve.

3

It Ain't Well Till Mommy Kisses It

A scream pierced the afternoon lull. Panic and pain edged the youthful voice. Steve threw down his newspaper and sprang to the front yard. When Aaron saw him he belted out between howls, "Go get my mother!"

As Jan headed toward the small figure sprawled on the asphalt, Steve said, "It's Aaron."

"I know." She nodded. All screams might sound the same to a father, but a mother knows which ones belong to her.

Steve tagged along to help, but Aaron didn't want his dad to see him hurt. He didn't want Dad to see the tears. He especially didn't want Dad to see the traces of blood on the scraped elbow.

Even at seven years old the boy wanted to be carried into the house by Mommy. He wanted her to take a damp cloth and wipe away the tears and dirt. He wanted her to bandage the elbow. He wanted her to hold him close and talk to him with that soft, caring voice. He wanted Mommy's kiss to let him know that the world was still OK and things would soon be back to normal.

Has anyone ever studied the scientific, medicinal value of this often miracle cure? No one's ever patented or advertised on television the healing in a mother's embrace. But every doctor and psychiatrist knows its value. Yet the scenario above goes unpracticed in millions of homes in America today. And our country suffers for it.

Never underestimate the healing power of a kiss and hug.

Pain frightens kids. The body seems to whirl out of control. It seems that the pain won't stop. What will happen next?

Blood frightens kids. You've got to have blood to live. Without it, you die, and death is scary. It's a state far away from friends and family and everything familiar.

Pain also frightens kids because it's associated with punishment. A child can't comprehend why he's being punished for skipping across the yard to chase a football.

What do Mom's kiss and hug and attention really do? The bandage will stop the bleeding, and time will take away the pain. But the kiss, and the hug, and the soft, kind words of comfort tell the child that someone's in control, someone's able to take care of the problem, someone loves and accepts him even in the midst of something gone wrong.

The anxiety soon gives way to peace, and that condition allows the body to concentrate wholly on healing the hurt or wound. And the body is very good at that when not distracted by other things. The body begins its mending process, and children are sure that Mommy's kiss had something to do with it.

They're right.

Hurts come in different shapes and sizes and types. The only thing we can count on is that our children will face their share. Here are just a few.

Physical hurts
- everyday pains such as bumps, scrapes, bruises, and bee stings
- everyday afflictions such as colds, flu, and sinus infections
- childhood diseases such as measles, chicken pox, and pink eye
- big catastrophes such as broken arms, stitches, and appendectomies

Emotional hurts
- when they lose games and friends
- when emotions cannot be contained ("I can't stop crying!")
- when they just don't like themselves ("I'm the fattest girl in my class.")

Social hurts
- lack of acceptance ("Carmen won't let me eat lunch at her table.")
- lack of skills ("How come I always sit on the sidelines when my soccer team plays?")
- lack of justice ("Just because Jason has a swimming pool, everybody's nice to him. It's not fair.")

Mental hurts
- frustration over lack of understanding ("Mother, I really tried to do this math homework—honest!")
- frustration over others ("I just don't understand how he could say such a thing about me.")
- frustration over self-image ("I'm such a klutz. I wish I had it together like Margie.")

Spiritual hurts
- seeking to understand God's plan ("Why can't Dad ever find a job?")
- seeking to understand their own role ("Does God want me to move to the jungle and be a missionary?")
- seeking to understand God's nature ("Is God punishing me for something I did wrong?")

Kids face a hurting world. As parents we will protect them from as many needless hurts as we can, but even more important we will show them how to survive when the hurts do come.

This is where good moms can play a key role.

WHAT TO DO WHEN YOUR CHILD HURTS

TAKE CARE OF PRIMARY PHYSICAL NEEDS

You have limitations, of course. Only a few mothers are trained nurses or doctors. But you can do more than provide bandages and Tylenol. You could take a first-aid course at a local college or Red Cross center. You can see that your house is properly stocked with supplies for minor emergencies. You can own and be familiar with first-aid books. You can read, clip, and save articles about treating household accidents. You can go over procedures for treating wounds, getting to the doctor, going to the emergency room of the hospital with your family before any emergency occurs. You can learn enough to know when you can be of some help and when you should get immediate professional attention. If at all possible, you should be there when a child is taken to the doctor or emergency room.

TAKE CARE OF SECONDARY PHYSICAL NEEDS

The scrape might be on the elbow, but the eyes need wiping, the nose needs tissue, the dirt on the face should be cleaned, the shoes need to be removed, the head placed on a pillow, or whatever. Sometimes the most serious injury is not the one that causes the most immediate pain. Examine the body. Comb the hair; get the glass of water; pull up the covers.

COMFORT WITH BOTH TOUCH AND WORDS

If the hurt is not physical but emotional, social, mental, or spiritual, you can begin here. Never underestimate the power of physical touch to bring comfort. Most hurting people want to be touched. Adults need an arm around the shoulder or a hand to hold. Children even more so. As Mom, you have the right to touch, and your child is used to your comforting hands. What about a child who doesn't want to be touched? Teach him how to accept your touch before his hurt comes along. Beyond that, respect his wishes to be left alone.

Aaron is by far the most active Bly boy. He whizzes through life with little time for things like sitting still for hugs from Mom. Anyway, that's the way he used to be. We noticed his aversion to hugging at an early age. So we decided to retrain him. Everyday for about three months each of us would make an effort to capture him for a few moments with a loving hug. He fought, squirmed, and complained, but we kept hugging. He got the idea. Soon it was Aaron who was initiating the affection.

"I haven't had my hug today," he'd fuss.

Last week Janet attended an out-of-town conference. Aaron was in bed asleep when she returned late one night. About an hour later we heard a polite knock at our bedroom door (a gentle habit he's picked up on his own). "Mommy, you forgot to hug me," he called. He's come a long way from the "don't touch me" days.

When a child is hurt, the tone of your voice becomes as important as the words themselves. Right at first they are really not concerned with the wisdom being given.

When Junior limps into the house with ripped jeans and bloody knees, you have a choice of diving right into your "I told you never to jump your bicycle off the curb" and "Why didn't you change into your old jeans after school?" discourse, or you could say say something like, "Tommy! What happened? Stay right there so I can get a good look at you."

Either way, he won't catch the words. He'll only hear the tone. Is it the carping of a lecture or the crooning of comfort? The comfort's what he needs right now. The lecture can come later, and to much better profit.

LISTEN TO WHAT HAPPENED AND TO WHAT HURTS

The more we listen, the more we know what the real problem is. But we're also providing a healthy environment in which a child can unleash his hurts and disappointments, which in itself is very therapeutic.

Andrea's the smartest girl in Sissy's class. When Sissy asked to be chosen to be on Andrea's team for the science project, Sissy received a note stating, "I don't want you on my team!" So Sissy collapses in tears at home.

"Why does Andrea feel that way?" Mom pries.

"Because she doesn't want any goody-goody church girls on her team, I guess," Sissy pouts.

Mom can then gently dig a little deeper. "What makes you think that?"

"She told Marcy she only wants girls who wear lipstick and pierce their ears," she fumes with a quick glare in Mom's direction.

But Mom's undeterred. "Is that really the whole reason?"

"It sure is—that and the fact I got a higher grade than her on the last math test." She pauses to smile. "I don't think anyone's ever done that to her before."

More than surface listening nudges out the complete story.

PRAY WITH THEM FOR GOD'S HELP

Ask God to bring healing. Always ask for the very best solution, then leave the provision to our all-wise heavenly Father. He has many avenues open to Him. He can work through doctors (who study His creation), through the natural healing strength of the body (which is His invention), or by instantaneous correction. In any case, He is the creator, sustainer, and healer. Your child needs to know that God cares about the hurts and that He is ready and willing to help.

Pray for the Lord's comfort. A soul is troubled, a mind confused, a spirit worried. God wants to bring His peace to their turmoil.

Isaiah 66:13 states, "As one whom his mother comforts, so I will comfort you."

Pray for understanding. Why did this happen? Why is she being treated this way? Why did he get hurt right before the big game? Why?

James 1:5 informs us that "if any of you lacks wisdom, let him ask of God, who gives to all men generously."

Pray for guidance. What should Sissy do now? How should she treat Andrea? What about those who side with Andrea? Should she change science classes? Ignore all of them? Get her ears pierced? Ask the Lord, together, to show you what to do.

Pray for the ability to allow God to use this present hurt in order to accomplish a meaningful purpose. Ask Him to teach others a lesson through this situation. Ask him to provide an open door into some other worthwhile activity.

This may be a time to point out to your child how God took even the horrible tragedy of the murder of Christ, His Son, to make a way for us to have the hope of eternal life. Such a God can be trusted to make something positive from the messes we hand Him.

Encourage your child to confess. If, indeed, part of the hurt results from personal actions, have him admit it in blunt, specific terms. "I'm sorry I disobeyed Daddy about leaving the spray paint cans alone." "I'm sorry I made Billy mad by calling him Shark Face." "I'm sorry I bragged about beating Andrea on the math test." Then reassure him of God's complete forgiveness.

EXPLAIN WHAT HAS HAPPENED AND WHAT WILL HAPPEN NEXT

Tell your children that the dab of flowing blood can cleanse the wound, then the skin will scab over and heal itself underneath before falling off. Help them understand why some kids are so insecure, why some lash out at others, why some are afraid of competition.

Help them to see that cruelty, jealousy, fear, and prejudice speak of deeper needs. Help them to see that there is a future, and advise them to keep this hurt in perspective.

TELL THEM OF YOUR OWN SIMILAR EXPERIENCES

Don't scare them with old horror stories, but let them know how frightened you were when you fell out of the tree and had to get fifteen stitches in your forehead or how you lost the election you just knew you would win.

Let them know that pain is helpful because it tells us something is wrong and we had better do something about it. Tell them about the time Susy Ferguson called you "tubby" during swim class and you didn't go to school for three days.

Sixteen-year-old Nanci stopped by Steve's office. "I'm kind of depressed," she blurted out. "I flunked my driving test."

"You seen to be handling it pretty well," he observed.

"Well, me and Mom had this long talk. Did you know she flunked her driving test two times? Hey, me and my mom are a lot alike."

"Is that OK?" he replied.

"Oh, yeah, my mom's really neat."

HELP THEM PLAN A COURSE OF ACTION
THAT MIGHT AVOID FUTURE PAIN

Do some new rules need to be made? Is there an example from the Bible that could help them find some direction?

The Bible can be amazingly practical, such as in the following story of King David.

David wouldn't allow his men to attack a man named Shimei when he called the King names (2 Samuel 16:5). "Perhaps the Lord is in this," David suggested to them (v. 12).

The responses that God always encourages are those that are within the bounds of His wisdom:

"The wisdom from above is first pure, then peaceable, gentle, reasonable, full of mercy and good fruits, unwavering, without hypocrisy" (James 3:17).

God allows pain to continue in the world for a purpose. We discover that purpose as we seek ways to triumph in the midst of trouble.

TAKE CARE OF ABANDONED ACTIVITIES, PEOPLE, AND EQUIPMENT

When they come flying through the door, often they've left behind an abandoned skateboard, some friends waiting their return, a jacket thrown in a neighbor's yard, or a missed appointment. The time comes to restore order. Mom may need to lead, help, or supervise.

RELEASE THEM BACK TO THEIR ACTIVITIES

This is sometimes harder than it sounds. Is the best thing to take away the bicycle, pull them out of that school, isolate them in a germ-free room, or refuse to let them participate in that activity ever again? There's a time to jump right back into the fray.

Good health is the best prevention for future illnesses. So it is with other injuries. When things are going well and there are no hurts, that's the time to strengthen kids for future experiences.

Build up their bodies with nutrition, rest, and exercise.

Build up their emotions with teaching self-control, priorities, and balanced self-acceptance.

Build up their relationships with teaching them how to forge lasting friendships, by clutching high standards while seeking always to understand.

Build up their minds with creative study, travel, and exploration.

Build up their spirits with consistent exposure to God's Word, friendship with other believers, and habitual worship and prayer.

Our Aaron carries a "hug license" in his wallet that claims a daily hug prescription: 4 hugs for survival, 8 hugs for maintenance, 12 hugs for growth. He points it out to us whenever he believes he's being neglected, which can even be on days when everything's right, he's feeling well, and no catastrophes are close at hand.

One day Janet teased him. "You got me just in time. I only have one hug left."

"Oh, no, you don't." He laughed. "You have thousands." Most of us do have the capacity for many times the hugs that we give out. Mothering begins at home, but it can expand to the many "orphans" around us—in the neighborhood, in the classroom—wherever our lives cross. Perhaps we can't house them, but we can take time to listen to some, maybe bandage a hurt for others, and to reach out and hug some.

Being a good mom might become a total life-style.

4

Who Likes It Besides Your Mother?

Suzi's drawing pictures. This one is a house and a tree. Or is it a house and a rabbit? Or a tree and a rabbit? It's hard to tell sometimes.

But Mom knows the difference.

Nobody on the face of the earth knows her child better than Mom. She still remembers when Suzi couldn't roll over in her crib, let alone hold a crayon and make vague attempts to scribble. She's made imaginary plans for Suzi's future success ever since and discussed her ability and talent with all who'd listen. And now, however gradually it starts, Suzi is beginning to show some signs of development. Mom can hardly wait to see what appears. She'll stand and cheer at every advancement.

Mothers should never stop cheering them on.

The large downtown church brimmed full of families ready to participate in the seminary graduation service. Right before the service began, an ambulance pulled up, and an attendant rolled a patient prone in a hospital bed down the aisle. A tube and bag hung above her.

At the end of the service each graduate was introduced by name as he received his diploma from the seminary president. As one particular young man marched across the platform, those of us nearby noticed the lady in the hospital bed prop herself up on one elbow and hoarsely whisper, "That's my boy, Leon! Thank you, Jesus!"

The whole crowd suddenly broke out in applause and tears for a heroic mom who wasn't ashamed to lead the cheering section for her Leon. We got the feeling that that wasn't the first time she had encouraged him. As long as there was breath in her body, it wouldn't be the last either.

Several prestigious awards were given out that night. We can't remember any of them, but we will never forget Leon's courageous mom.

Here are two quick clues to keeping your motherly praise within bounds.

Speak from the heart. Your mind can tell you that the picture lacks much in the way of color, balance, perspective, neatness, form, or shape. Your mind can tell you that Mrs. Miller's little Samuel can draw better. But don't worry. Our children have a whole world full of critics who speak from the mind. What they really need is one person who'll react from the heart.

What's your heart's view of the project? Let the critical side of your brain be tempered by an overall impression of potential, effort, and attitude.

Let your praise be constructive encouragement for future achievements. Don't say, "Oh, that's very nice, but I bet you could do better next time." That implies you consider the present work substandard. Rather say, "Wow, you're getting so good at drawing trees and houses, I'll bet you'll be drawing flowers and bunnies in no time at all!"

Sure enough, next Friday, after nine weeks of nothing but trees and houses, here comes a picture of bunnies and flowers. When Junior is ready, Mom is always there to encourage higher goals and greater achievements.

Mary, the mother of Jesus, was an encourager.

Those early hectic days in Bethlehem swelled with visitors and pronouncements, but she remembered them all.

"Mary treasured up all these things, pondering them in her heart" (Luke 2:19).

What did she have to ponder?

How about when the angel told her that her son "will be great, and will be called the Son of the Most High; and the Lord God will give Him the throne of His father David; and He will reign over the house of Jacob forever; and His kingdom will have no end" (Luke 1:32,33)?

How about the shepherds' report that they heard this One is "the Savior, who is Christ the Lord" (Luke 2:11)?

How about the comment of the wise men about following a great star to where they resided (Matthew 2:11)?

Then there were the words of Simeon: "Behold, this Child is appointed for the fall and rise of many in Israel, and for a sign to be opposed—and a sword will pierce even your own soul—to the end that thoughts from many hearts may be revealed" (Luke 2:34-35).

And the response of Anna: "And at that very moment she came up and began giving thanks to God, and continued to speak of Him to all those who were looking for the redemption of Jerusalem" (Luke 2:38).

Can you imagine how such words shaped Mary's plans and dreams and ideas of the future for her son? He had barely begun His preaching ministry when they attended a wedding in Cana of Galilee. When Mary noticed the plight of the embarrassed host, she blurted out, "Jesus, they have no wine" (John 2:3). This shortage may have even been due to the crowd that had begun to follow Jesus around.

Her plans for His life included His solving such a practical problem. However, this request didn't fit His plans. "Woman, what do I have to do with you?" He replied (John 2:4). But Jesus did comply with the request in His own private way.

Was Mary being too pushy? Maybe. She acted just like a mother who is anxious to see her child perform according to his gifts and talents. Certainly, her concern didn't strain the relationship. Some of those last chosen words Jesus spoke from the discomfort of the cross guaranteed that His mother would be properly taken care of after His death (John 19:26-27).

How can a mother act as a cheerleader and encourage her children to strive for their best, without being overly aggressive? Here are some suggestions.

ENCOURAGEMENT GUIDELINES

SET QUALITY GOALS FOR YOURSELF

Let them see you aim for a worthy pursuit, meet some special need, or develop a new skill.

Darla, at thirty-eight, is taking a Spanish class at the community college. She wants to learn the language well enough to teach a backyard Bible class in the Hispanic section of town.

Patty's memorizing the whole book of Philippians. She works on it a few verses at a time while her kids practice their own memory verses.

After twelve years of singing in the choir, Shirleen is taking voice lessons. "They scare me to death," she says, "but how else will I get any better?"

Pushing little Junior and Sissy out into fields and situations that no other family member has ever faced is a difficult task. But when they see you doing similar things, well, after all, then it's a family tradition.

LET THEM DREAM THEIR OWN DREAMS

Cowboys, firemen, and football players—those are the dreams of many little boys when they're four to eight. Sometime in the process they will want to be just like Daddy. But those ideas give way to peer pressure. Then they'll want to be astronauts or multimillion dollar computer designers or both.

Poor kids can grow up to be neurosurgeons. Bashful kids can wind up as actors. Rural kids can learn industrial design. Urban kids can learn to ride and rope horses. Girls can aim for Supreme Court justice. Farm boys can learn to write books.

Encourage them to have big dreams, even though some goals may seem unrealistic or farfetched. Your child's chances of becoming a famous movie or television star before he reaches the age of twelve may seem extremely remote, unless a close relative happens to be an actor, director, or producer. And you may have sincere moral qualms about such a choice. But conflict with most dreams and goals focuses on differences of opinion.

Be wary of smashing young dreams because of your own lack of interest or lack of faith. Help them to see that with God directing and enabling them, "nothing will be impossible" (Luke 1:37).

PROVIDE THEM ROOM TO EXPLORE

So they want to try piano lessons this year and archery lessons next year. If it's at all financially possible, let them try. If they're excited about tennis camp, computer camp, weight-loss camp, or woodcarving camp, send them. Load them up and take them to zoos, science fairs, museums, trade shows, and rodeos.

Spend time watching and discussing with them some of the well done shows on the local educational television channel.

Plan vacations that do more than tour pizza joints and amusement parks. Travel to different states, look at varieties of scenery, attempt an adventure or two. Watch the Indians make turquoise jewelry in Arizona, the old timers blow glass in New England, and air traffic controllers guide planes in Chicago.

It may be true that some of these investments will go nowhere, but along the way they may pick up the courage and initiative to try new things.

Ten years ago we bought Russ a guitar. Now it's relegated to the closet. Then we provided Mike a deluxe thirty-five millimeter camera and a New York correspondence school photography course. That lasted three months. At another time there was the computer, disk drive, printer, desk, and programs investment. That project endured three years.

But there was also the year Russ received a set of oil paints and some canvas. You should see the artist now. Oils, water colors, pastels, charcoal—you name it. Our walls are covered. He's really good. We can tell you that straight from the heart.

Never mind the things that didn't work out. They had an opportunity to explore. We're glad we gave them the chance.

EXPOSE THEM TO OTHER DREAMERS

Ideas and thoughts about future goals fascinate exploring minds. Rubbing shoulders with people who are actually doing such things is downright contagious.

Bobby wants to be a fireman? Take him to a firehouse and let him talk to the captain. "We're just little kids who love to put out fires," one recently told me.

Your twelve-year-old Sissy wants to be a scientist? Take her to visit with the folks at M.I.T. or Cal. Tech. or the nearest observatory.

Billy wants to play pro basketball? Find out how to snag some tickets right behind the home team's bench.

You might not know much about the subject in which they're currently interested, but chances are there is someone around who does. If not, take them to the library and let them check out books on the topic.

You don't want them to turn out just the same as someone else, but maybe they will learn to dream. "If she could set out to become the world's best gymnast at age sixteen, then maybe I could make the Olympics in swimming," they may muse.

Too many kids never even consider any of the possibilities.

HELP THEM ACHIEVE THEIR GOAL

Your children need to know they're not alone.

A couple of years back a fourteen-year-old girl won the world's championship in barrel racing. That's a sport where you race your horse in a clover-leaf pattern around three barrels. It happens to be just about the only event open to females at most rodeos. This young lady won the title again when she was fifteen and sixteen. In order to win the world champion title she had to win more money than anyone else in that event. That meant she had to enter rodeos about every weekend of the year. Some weeks she may have entered two or three.

Now we don't personally know this young lady or her parents. But we can guarantee you that they are a couple of dedicated folks, because we know someone has to load up that horse every week and drive all night through the Texas panhandle to make sure the rider gets to the next day's competition.

Moms have traditionally played a crucial part in helping kids achieve their dreams. That's why academy award winners, football quarterbacks, and successful politicians all grin into the camera and say, "Thanks, Mom."

REMIND THEM THAT YOUR LOVE IS NOT
DEPENDENT UPON THEIR SUCCESS

There is a difference between pushy mothers and helpful mothers.

Helpful mothers are at peace with themselves and trust God's plan for their children's lives. Pushy mothers feel cheated or driven and try to gain some imagined loss through the fulfillments of their offspring.

Helpful mothers see their children as grand opportunities to learn more about our world through their perceptive young eyes. Pushy mothers always know what's best for their children, no matter what their ages.

Helpful mothers see a bigger picture than do the neighbors or other bystanders. Pushy mothers use their kids to achieve social acceptance or power.

Cheering Them On

THINGS TO DO

If Mom's going to be the number one fan, what are some practical ways to encourage each child? Here are three suggestions that can be enacted immediately and practiced daily:

Honestly compliment your child at least once a day. Thank your child for putting away his bike or politely answering the front door. Let your child know that you appreciate the way he got dressed all by himself or the way he mowed the lawn or how pretty she looked in the pink sweater. He might not acknowledge the compliment. He might act as if you never said it. But it is doing its appointed job nonetheless. He can never forget that at least one person on this earth thinks he is something special and notices his efforts.

Continually expect from your child the best, highest, noblest response. "Mom always expects me to do it right." That knowledge has influenced countless consciences as mother's responses are anticipated, whether she's nearby or not. Make a habit of letting your children know what you anticipate their decisions to be in specific situations.

Teach your child God's ways through the spontaneous and commonplace. As you open your child's curtains in the morning proclaim, "The Lord sure made a beautiful day today!"

At breakfast you might ask, "Well, I wonder what kind of surprises God has in store for us today?"

Let talk about the world from God's point of view flow naturally from the circumstances of any given moment. The Bible explains this type of positive religious training way back in the Old Testament.

"And these words, which I am commanding you today, shall be on your heart; and you shall teach them diligently to your sons and shall talk of them when you sit in your house and when you walk by the way and when you lie down and when you rise up" (Deuteronomy 6:6-7).

THINGS TO AVOID

There are certain established noes that all good moms will want to avoid.

Don't compare a child's work with a sibling's. As a rule, Junior is not motivated—in any good sense—by hearing that his cursive letters are not as neat and straight as Sissy's. Equating Junior's style of writing to Sissy's could be as ridiculous as comparing silk slippers to skateboards.

Don't initiate discussion of a child's failures in front of other family members. Allow your child to bring up trials and tribulations if he so chooses. If he doesn't, keep them a confidential matter between the two of you. This can build trust and confidence that could be profitable in a future crisis of even greater importance. He won't be afraid to come to Mom to discuss private turmoils. You can provide a safe haven in a world that seems to take thoughtless potshots at him.

Don't make light of a child's dreams and ideas. Twelve-year-old Jesus discussed the law with the Temple teachers to the amazement of His parents. "And His mother treasured all these things in her heart" (Luke 2:42-52).

The lad Joseph told of visions that he would one day rule over his elder brothers and father (Genesis 37:1-10).

Young Samuel "ministered to the Lord," and though "word from the Lord was rare in those days," and "visions were infrequent," Samuel heard God speak to him (1 Samuel 3).

Some dreams evolve out of the human mind, and others spring from the inspiration of God's Spirit. A child needs to learn how to discern one from the other. So does a mom.

"When you are in the dark, listen, don't talk," advises Oswald Chambers. "When you open your mouth in the dark, you will talk in the wrong mood."

Great counsel for moms when their children spin tales that might seem strange or farfetched.

These may be times to "keep watching and praying" (Matthew 26:41).

DON'T FORGET DAD

Kids aren't the only family members needing encouragement from moms. Dads need it too. There's still a lot of kid in him as well. He has his share of dreams, ideas, plans, confrontations, victories, and successes. He needs a cheerleader too—one who'll rally the gang to his side.

Brag about Dad in public. Do this where he can hear, especially in front of the kids or his parents or some other significant someone such as a friend, employer, or coworker. Be open with your honest feelings about his accomplishments, especially when you're irritated with some fault.

Remind the kids of how hard Dad works. One of Janet's favorite phrases to Russ and Mike when Steve worked on the farm was "Whooee, do we ever have a hard working Dad." She said it half in fun and half as a nudge of respect for their father's efforts.

Listen to Dad's gripes. Don't immediately remind him that you have plenty of troubles of your own. Care about his conflicts and frustrations.

Let Dad dream. When he reads about capturing wild horses in Ne-vada, drag out the maps, trace the plains and trails with him, and say, "I bet you'd make one great cowboy."

Assure Dad that he and the kids are priorities. Everything else—from the house, to your career, or simply the evening's plans—can come and go. You're not clutching anything but the Lord, your husband, and your children.

Support Dad's special interests. Buy him the tools or the books or bring him the travel brochures. Make room in the den for his table or shelf or display rack. Save relevant articles, or go with him to that concert or trade show.

Seek the Lord on his behalf. Let him know you pray for him and ask God's protection and wisdom for him in all his ventures. If he is open, tuck your hands in his and ask God's blessing on his day before he leaves for work.

Show Dad public affection. Depending on his preference, either hug him, kiss him, greet him with fond words, or just lightly touch his arm. Allow him the pride of showing others that his wife's crazy about him and isn't ashamed to let the world know it.

Knock Dad's socks off once in a while. Pack up a picnic lunch, pick him up at work, and drive to the beach, the woods, or the nearest park. Another time tell him you bought two tickets to the motorcy-cle races and you're looking for someone to go with you. Or perhaps digging into that long-standing mess in the guest room or sewing the buttons on his shirts will do the same trick.

Good moms keep right on leading the cheers, no matter what the age of the kids or who belittles her attention. "Well, who likes it be-sides your mother?" the familiar joke goes. Even so, right into adult-hood, grownup kids never seem to outgrow that inner desire to know "what does Mom think about it?"

5

If It Weren't for Momma's Prayers

Little boys are drawn to stray dogs. Twelve-year-old girls are crazy about horses. Any kid will choose chocolate pie over custard. Whatever Sissy wants, everyone in school already has one. The pants that Junior rips will always be his newest pair. Moms pray for their kids.

There are some things in life you can count on. Call them the facts of family life. Everyone knows that mothers are supposed to pray for their children. It's there in the job description somewhere, isn't it?

It must be, because more good is attributed to the effect of Momma's prayers than nearly any other power source in history.

"If it weren't for my praying mother, I don't know where I'd be today." We hear it so often it sounds like a cliché.

Not all moms pray for their kids, of course, but that doesn't mean they don't love them. Some moms just don't know anything about real prayer. For various reasons they've never considered the claims of Jesus seriously enough to trust Him as their Savior, Lord, and Guide. Without that active step of faith, there's no incentive for faithful, fervent prayer. God is either assumed to be a myth or a vague, unknowable deity "way out there somewhere." Either way, He has no relevance to them in the nitty-gritty of day-by-day pressures and cares.

We all have different religious upbringings. We all have different spiritual pilgrimages as well. By whatever route or means, those who receive Christ also receive God's Holy Spirit, and He creates within us a drive to pray on behalf of those we love, to seek His daily protection, help, and insight. Non-Christian moms may pray, too, but probably only in times of crisis, and God may be quickly forgotten when the crisis ends. That is, unless the overwhelming burden of mothering forces them to reconsider their spiritual commitment. That's what happened to Janet:

"Mike, our second child, had just been born, and the added responsibilities made me panic. What did I know about parenting? How could I help my children find their way through this uncertain, sometimes violent, world? I hardly knew the way myself.

"I often thought about God. I longed to know if He really existed. If He did, what was He like? In my early teens I sometimes attended church with neighbors. A small black Bible a Sunday school teacher gave me back then had remained unopened for years. I wasn't even sure where it was.

"One day I searched through the bookcase and dug around in a hope chest and several junk drawers hoping to find that Bible. No sign of it. The more frustrated my quest became, the more I imagined it to hold the mysterious answers to all my questions. To my sheer delight I finally found it at the bottom of a box of textbooks in the garage.

"I ran into the house, plopped onto the couch, and opened the pages to Genesis, 'In the beginning God created the heaven and the earth—'

"Several hours later my mind whirled. I never dreamed the Bible could be so exciting. It brimmed with people who knew God, who walked with Him, who talked with Him. For days I devoured page after page.

"Some months later Steve and I joined a Navigators home Bible study through a church fellowship. One night our Bible study leader asked us, 'Do you know for a fact that you have eternal life?' The question nearly knocked the breath from me. I knew the time for study and debate had ended. Either I believed God had come to earth in the form of Jesus Christ to die for my sins or I did not. Later that night I studied again the verses that both plagued and intrigued me: 'But as many as received Him, to them He gave the right to become children of God, even to those who believe in His name' (John 1:12). 'If you confess with your mouth Jesus as Lord, and believe in your heart that God raised Him from the dead, you shall be saved' (Romans 10:9).

"Finally, I took the plunge of betting my life that these words were gospel truth. That was twenty years ago, and I've never regretted that decision. In fact, each year seems to bring firmer proofs that the step taken that night was the smartest thing I ever did."

Steve's decision for Christ soon followed. Our conversions to Christ dramatically changed our approach to raising our family. For one thing, we began including God in each day-to-day situation and decision. That meant learning to pray. Before, without prayer, our family drifted, with very serious limitations. Without Christ we had no avenue for reaching God's ear, even if we cried out to Him.

Now we had the great desire and the right to approach God's throne at any time. However, one enemy has consistently reared its head in preventing faithful attention to this task. That enemy is *time*. It doesn't seem to matter whether a mother works at home or outside the home, whether she lives downtown or out in the hills, whether her home has five bathrooms or an outhouse in the back, she will fight for that quality time to pray.

FINDING TIME FOR PRAYER

Solving the problem of finding time for prayer is much more difficult than identifying it, but here are three suggestions that stretch the possibilities for more than "on the run" prayers.

GET UP EARLIER

It sounds dreary just to write those words down on paper. It sounds like a cheap shot at an exhausted mom, right? We know that 99 percent of the women we talk to claim, "I'm just not an early morning person." Others groan, "I spent half the night tending sick kids." Well, no one ever claimed that a strong prayer life would be easy —just extremely worthwhile and necessary.

For one thing, just fifteen minutes earlier would produce amazing results. All you need is the motivation. Admit it, if your husband came home and announced, "Hey, I've got two tickets for a week long vacation in Hawaii, but you'll have to rise half an hour earlier than usual to catch that plane on time," what would your response be? It's called finding the proper stimulus.

TRY DEPARTURE PRAYER

If you stay at home during the day, set aside the first fifteen minutes after the last child leaves. Unplug the telephone, refuse to answer the door, go into a back room, and pray. If you commute to work, use the travel time to offer intercessions for your family. You can carry your prayer list with you on the train, or tack it to the sun visor of your car. If you arrive at work early, complete your prayers in the parking lot.

SACRIFICE LUNCH

You can still eat a nourishing bite at lunch but arrange your time so that you have at least fifteen minutes alone. If necessary, eat at the park, in your car, out on the patio or balcony, or right in your kitchen. Those prayers for your family are just as vital as food is to your body. You must find the time somewhere.

If You Don't Pray, Who Will?

Are you counting on the pastor to remember your children? Do you assume that their Sunday school teachers are praying for them? But those busy people have so many to remember. They can't put the same degree of emphasis on your children that you can.

The only one you can be sure of is you. You must pray. Here are some of the reasons.

OUR STRUGGLES ARE SPIRITUAL

All the real struggles in this world are spiritual. "For our struggle is not against flesh and blood, but against the rulers, against the powers, against the world forces of this darkness, against the spiritual forces of wickedness in the heavenly places" (Ephesians 6:12).

Spiritual battles can only be fought with prayer. It's not merely the unpleasant little girl down the street that Sissy has to watch out for. It's not just a humanistic educational system that threatens Junior. An eternal war for our children's very souls rages. We can't afford to be so naive as to think we're immune to those conflicts.

KIDS WON'T PRAY FOR THEMSELVES

Chances are your children won't remember to pray for themselves. Most children have a hard enough time remembering to bring their coats home from school, to not slam the front door, and to keep the television turned down. They sure won't be consistent in prayer. We certainly can't expect another family member to be more disciplined than we are. If it takes a near miraculous act of strength and concentration for moms to find time to pray, think of how much more difficult it will be for anyone less motivated.

PRAYER GETS RESULTS

Prayer opens up new possibilities. "The effective prayer of a righteous man [or woman] can accomplish much" (James 5:16).

"The Lord has heard my supplication. The Lord receives my prayer" (Psalm 6:9).

"O Lord, Thou has heard the desire of the humble, Thou wilt strengthen their heart, Thou wilt incline Thine ear" (Psalm 10:17).

"In my distress I called upon the Lord, and cried to my God for help; He heard my voice out of His temple, and my cry for help before Him came into His ears" (Psalm 18:6).

"This poor man cried and the Lord heard him, and saved him out of all his troubles" (Psalm 34:6).

"I waited patiently for the Lord; and He inclined to me, and heard my cry" (Psalm 40:1).

WAYS TO PRAY

Each family member has very specific needs that a mother wants to remember, however there are always general topics to keep before God's attention too.

PRAY FOR THEIR HEALTH AND SAFETY

We sometimes seem to live in a "Russian roulette" world. In a closed-quarters classroom of twenty-eight disease-prone children, Junior is sure to catch a bug eventually. In an environment overrun by tons of motor-driven metal, he faces a major hazard crossing the street. One weak moment of temptation could lead a young mind into an incapacitating battle with substance abuse, an outbreak of bizarre and violent behavior, or worse.

Pray for God's hedge of protection around each child and for His measure of courage and wisdom for each day's particular stresses.

PRAY FOR THEIR PHYSICAL AND MENTAL ADVANCEMENT

Ask God to help them with the trauma of growing up, whatever that means for each child. Pray that their understanding of themselves will grow at the same rate as their bodies. Pray that they will feel comfortable with the physical changes that come. Pray for their knowledge to increase, as well as their wisdom. Wisdom is knowing the right thing to do with a particular bit of knowledge.

PRAY FOR THEIR SPIRITUAL ADVANCEMENT

Consider, honestly, where they are in their spiritual lives. Pray for them to understand God better. Pray that they will think of Him often. Pray for their personal commitment to Him. Pray that they will have an increasing desire to read God's Word. Pray for them to increase their attempt to live a life in obedience to the Lord's commands. Pray that they will be able to resist temptation. Pray for them to have opportunities to share their spiritual knowledge with others.

PRAY FOR TRUE ABUNDANCE IN THEIR LIVES

When Jesus promised us abundance (John 10:10), He included the young too. Abundance means a life with purpose, meaning, joy, and satisfaction. Pray that your children's daily routine is satisfying. Pray that the joy will be more than just surface smiles or temporary laughter but will be lodged deep within. Pray that they will feel they are a part of what God is doing in this world.

PRAY FOR THEIR FRIENDS

Kids select playmates very casually—often based on whoever is available. Yet what those friends say and do greatly affects their own behavior.

The Bible says, "Even a child is known by his doings, whether his work be pure, and whether it be right" (Proverbs 20:11, KJV*).

Pray for each friend by name.

PRAY FOR THEIR FUTURE SPOUSES

Whether your child is three months, three years, thirteen years, or thirty years old, pray for his or her future marital partner. Pray that he or she will make a lifetime, permanent commitment to the marriage. Pray that he or she will openly acknowledge Christ as Savior and Lord. Pray that the future spouse will have the qualities and temperament to bring out the best in your child.

PRAY FOR THEIR SELF-ACCEPTANCE

Pray that your children will like being who they are and will be freed from the slavery of always comparing themselves to others. Pray they will have a healthy balance of self-confidence by recognizing their importance to God, to you, and to their community. Pray that they will accept their present age, mental ability, and skill level and will find contentment in each day's activities.

PRAY FOR THEM TO DEVELOP A BIG VISION

Who knows what God may have in store for them? That preparation begins now. Pray that they will learn to look beyond the immediate to see how today's actions affect tomorrow. Pray for just the right challenges to come their way.

PRAY FOR PEACE WITH SIBLINGS

"Behold, how good and how pleasant it is for brothers to dwell together in unity!" (Psalm 133:1).

*King James Version.

Pray that in the midst of the squabbles they will grow in their appreciation of one another, to see how much alike they are and how valuable their differences can be.

Some kids are harder to pray for than others. But then, some kids are plain harder to raise than others. Some take every ounce of your courage, wisdom, and sanity. The Bible readily admits that there will be children like that.

"A foolish son is a grief to his mother" (Proverbs 10:1).

"A foolish man despises his mother" (Proverbs 15:20).

"He who assaults his father and drives his mother away is a shameful and disgraceful son" (Proverbs 19:26).

"He who curses his father or his mother, his lamp will go out in time of darkness" (Proverbs 20:20).

"The rod and reproof give wisdom, but a child who gets his own way brings shame to his mother" (Proverbs 29:15).

There is an "eye that mocks a father, and scorns a mother" (Proverbs 30:17).

It's difficult to know how to pray for a problem child. In addition to the suggestions already mentioned, you might try the following:

1. Pray that God will use the present difficulties to accomplish His best in the child's life.

2. Pray that the struggles the child is now facing will lead to the discovery of the hidden hurts that cause such behavior.

3. Pray that Satan will not gain control of his life, especially during this time of rebellion.

4. Pray that every painful lesson will be a tool for helping others in the future.

5. Pray for others around him who could be hurt during his rebellion. The innocent often suffer when a prodigal roams from home.

6. Finally, pray that you will not grow weary of praying for him. Pledge yourself to pray as long as it takes.

Good moms always care. Christian moms will pray. Moms with troubled kids will never stop praying.

6

There's Nothing Like
a Plate of Warm Cookies

When Denise was nine years old a car hit her kitten. As soon as the tears subsided, her mom ushered her into the sweet smelling kitchen. She plopped down on a stool while Mom brought out a plate of warm chocolate chip cookies and a glass of icy cold milk. Oh, it didn't take away all the sorrow, but it sure helped.

At age fourteen, none of the boys at Hoover High School asked her to the freshman class social. She burst through the door of the house and left a trail of tears clear into her bedroom. About half an hour later she heard a knock. When she opened her door, no one was there, but on the floor sat a plate of steaming chocolate chip cookies, a big glass of milk, and an attached note that said, "I love you." She wasn't sure that the following lonely Friday night passed any faster, but she appreciated the momentary diversion.

When Denise turned eighteen, she backed the family car over her little brother's bicycle. For nearly an hour she stood alone in the living room with her father as he lectured her on everything from the cost of living, to carelessness, to the pitfalls of rock music. Finally, her mother intervened. "He's right, Denise. Now, get in there right now and show some responsibility by washing the dishes."

In the kitchen a huge pile of dirty dishes awaited her. But one particular dish caught her eye. There, next to Mom's stool, sat the plate of warm cookies and a glass of milk. They were, in her memory, perhaps the best her mother had ever baked.

Denise is twenty-four now. Last Friday she was passed over for the promotion at the insurance agency. She took it hard. Back at her small condo she sprawled on the couch and stared at the wall. Several times she reached for the phone but then drew back. After all, she was grown now, on her own, independent. She could take it. The living room stood in total darkness when she finally dialed. "Mom? Hi, it's me. Listen, can I have that great recipe of yours for chocolate chip cookies? What do you mean, what's wrong? Nothing's wrong. Really? Does it show that much?"

Some folks would call it spoiling your kids. We all know of brats, no matter what their age, who get everything they whine for. That's unhealthy parenting. On the other hand, a little spoiling once in a while never hurt anyone.

Justice could be defined as getting exactly what you deserve. But justice isn't always found. We are often treated unfairly and have no option but to sit and take it.

Ah, but then those rare, royal moments when we're treated better than we deserve really shine out. Moms are the likeliest candidates for providing such moments.

But there are some cautions to giving a child better than he deserves.

Don't do it if it means that sin will go unconfessed. That's the kind of spoiling talked about in Proverbs 29:15: "The rod and reproof give wisdom, but a child who gets his own way brings shame to his mother."

When correction is the chief goal, a child can't go his own way unchecked. He should learn to admit mistakes and not gloss them over.

Don't do it if it means interfering with God's plan. Rebekah was about to give birth to twins. She sought the Lord's wisdom and was told, among other things, that "the older shall serve the younger" (Genesis 25:23). We are not told whether she mentioned these words to Isaac. He acted as if he was ignorant of the prediction. As was the custom, Isaac favored Esau, his oldest son. But Rebekah "loved Jacob" (v. 28)—the younger.

When the boys grew up, Isaac, nearly blind, prepared to give his patriarchal blessing. Rebekah seized the opportunity to maneuver her favorite, Jacob, into Isaac's favor through deception. God did not need such a scheme to carry out His plans. Rebekah's kind of spoiling generated much grief for them all.

Don't do it if it means others must be treated unjustly. Jesus told of a way that one could show mercy without harming others.

A vineyard owner hired some needy workers at daybreak for the wages of one denarius for a day's work. They were delighted. Later, the owner encountered some men at the marketplace and hired them too for the same pay. Even later in the afternoon he hired more men. An hour before quitting time, he acquired his last laborers.

When the time came to collect their wages, those who had worked all day were surprised that the part-timers got paid the same denarii. "Well, then, maybe we'll receive even more," they reasoned. But they were disappointed to find out that they got only the denarii they'd been promised. They immediately complained. However, the owner of the vineyard defended his actions. In effect he explained that all the workers needed the full pay to care for their families, and if he chose to spoil the latecomers by giving them equal pay, that was his business (see Matthew 20:1-16).

How to Make Them Feel Special
Without Turning Them into Brats

We noticed the following sign hanging on the wall of a first grade classroom: "Your mother does not work here. Clean up your own mess."

As much as we *want* to show that extra special attention to our children, or, in some cases, believe that we *must* in order to be a good mom, our spoiling will always appear as too much coddling to someone else—a schoolteacher with thirty other charges, for instance. As they grow older and reach out into the real world, our children may be shocked to discover that no one else feels quite the same imperative to pander to their needs that Mom does. A good mom will keep that in mind as she indulges in spoiling. Parcel out your indulgences with care.

GIVE THEM FOOD

Clear a corner of a cupboard somewhere to stock up on supplies of their favorite goodies. No one's allowed to touch the ingredients. They're a reserve supply for a very special occasion. Mom alone knows when the occasion is special enough. What does it mean? It means that someone was thinking of them all afternoon. It means someone did something for them that didn't have to be done. It means they're loved.

The prophet Elijah was pulled out of a deep panic by a similar means. He ran for his life when Jezebel threatened to kill him. When he didn't know where else to hide he cried out to God, "O Lord, take my life!" God ignored this request and replied, "Arise, eat."

In the strength of the food that God provided, Elijah traveled for forty more days and nights (1 Kings 19).

GIVE THEM YOUR TIME

Set down the project on which you're so intent, and look them in the eye. That designates undivided attention. Then, really listen so they don't have to repeat themselves (something our Aaron detests).

Go outside and play catch because everybody else is gone or busy. Force a smile when they chide, "Ah, Mom, where'd ya learn to throw like that?"

Read *Go, Dog, Go* for the one hundredth time without skipping any words or pages.

Don't insist that these times must always be designated by you. If it's not their idea, don't be perturbed if they aren't too excited. "But I'm right in the middle of watching Inspector Gadget!"

GIVE THEM ALTERNATIVES

Not every mom has the knack of creatively detouring a child's mind away from failure, loneliness, depression, and the like. In fact, our attempts may seem to just rub salt in the wound. This special craft can be learned, however, by practice and by observing other mothers who do it well. "How delightful is a timely word," says Proverbs 15:23.

When Sissy doesn't make the cheerleading squad, spell out the virtues of trying for the drill team instead.

When it rains the night Junior wanted to pitch the tent in the backyard, make a comfy place for him in the garage.

GIVE THEM A SURPRISE

Around our house we've lost the meaning of the term *surprise*. When Mom and Dad travel to a conference or speaking trip, Aaron always says, "Bring me back a surprise." Then he rattles off all his choices. They are clearly not surprises.

A real surprise is something totally out of your normal routine, something considered out of character for you. If you normally squat in the bleachers without so much as a peep during the volleyball game, next time furl out a four foot sign that says, "Spike 'em, Number 22." If you did that every week it wouldn't be a big deal. Do it just once, and it becomes a lifelong memory.

GIVE THEM ANOTHER CHANCE

Junior agreed to rake the lawn for two dollars. But he left his coat at school, so first he had to ride his bike back to retrieve it. Since the room was locked, he looked all over for the custodian. When he finally got the coat and headed home, he noticed a flat tire.

He pushed the bike to the service station and, by the time he returned home, dinner was ready. After dinner it was too dark to begin his chore. He's totally frustrated because he needed that two dollars in order to go roller skating with his buddy Ray tomorrow. What would you do?

If Junior had remembered his coat in the first place, as you warned him to do before he left for school, there would have been no problem. He brought the disappointment on himself. He should understand that. Then, perhaps, you may choose to spoil him. Give him a little more time to rake the leaves.

GIVE THEM A LAUGH

Lighten up.

Junior has just paraded through the living room wearing (or abusing) Sissy's new heels and doing a parody of how she acts right before a date. Give him the lecture about the sanctity of Sissy's belongings. Show him how he could have damaged the expensive shoes. Let him know the consequences if he does it again. *Then,* give him a laugh and tell him he really does do a good imitation of Sissy.

Infractions are punished. Commitments are kept. Justice will rule. But in the midst of all the legalities of family living, there's still time to smile and chuckle.

GIVE THEM A HUG

We never tire of hearing of Jesus' story about the prodigal son and the forgiving father (Luke 15:11-32). Here comes the son, dragging himself home a miserable failure. He does not deserve to be accepted. He does not deserve to be welcomed. And he certainly does not deserve a hug. But that's what he gets, along with a celebration in his honor.

Many claim, right along with the elder brother, that the old man was shamefully spoiling the kid. If that's true, then spoiling must be an acceptable heavenly practice in some cases, because Jesus gave the parable as an example of God's fatherly attention to His children.

If our children earn hugs only when they succeed or are good, we teach them that our love is conditional on performance. That is not love at all but merely a reward. Hugs come because these children belong to you, not because they're perfect.

But a word of caution is needed here. It's possible to spoil children in order to manipulate them or the situation to a parent's advantage. Then, ironically, spoiling becomes counterproductive. Watch for the danger signs.

The good guy/bad guy image. Daddy punishes; Mommy rewards. Daddy demands; Mommy lets you off. Daddy prohibits; Mommy permits ("But don't tell your father"). The purpose of this type of spoiling is to maintain a competitive position as the parent who really loves them, the one who has their best interests in mind. You are trying to line up loyalty among the troops just in case someday everyone needs to take sides.

To get even with a spouse. Divorced parents often fall into this trap. Buy Junior something that the other can't (or won't) buy in order to build points with the child. The purchased object or promised project becomes a wedge of conflict and barter between the opposing adults.

To impress your peers. "If you're really good at Mrs. Erickson's then Mommy will take you to the doughnut shop on the way home, and you can have a strawberry swirl." Translated that means, "If Jo Erickson knew my kids were little terrors sometime, I'd never live it down. After all, she received the Mother of the Year Award from the City Council, and she knows I led the protest against that 'R' rated movie they wanted to show at the Junior High last year. We've got to make a good showing for this lady."

In these situations we might as well stop at Rent-A-Kid and pay big bucks for the deluxe robot model.

To make life easier for yourself. "Oh, I know I said something about working with you on that new dress pattern tonight, but I've got a better idea. Why don't we go over to the mall tomorrow and buy you a dress instead? It would be so much easier."

"But, Mom, I want this style, and this material, and you promised to show me how to work all those extra dials—"

God's plan for mankind seems to allow for some spoiling.

Oh, yes, we are responsible for our own sin. And we deserved to pay the full, just penalty. But God provided His very own precious Son to bear our punishment and die in our place. He didn't have to do that. He would have been completely justified to allow us to keep to our path of total destruction.

The Bible calls this "grace," a huge, complex spiritual concept that's brought down to earth in understandable terms by a plate of undeserved chocolate chip cookies and a mom with a bent toward spoiling us—just a little.

7

Don't Talk That Way
in Front of Your Mother

Larry sat motionless in the corner of the barber shop, craning his neck to see around his father. In the barber's chair sat one of the biggest men he had ever seen. In a voice that boomed like a cannon, the man was telling about a recent hunting accident. His sentences were laced with profanity. Larry glanced at his dad for a reaction, but his dad seemed engrossed in his newspaper.

Then in the middle of a graphic sentence, the big man stopped talking. Larry followed the man's sheepish glance to the front door where Mrs. Lowrey and little Norman had just entered. The conversation immediately changed to a polite discussion of the new city park.

When the big man left, Larry asked his dad, "How come he stopped in the middle of his story?"

"Oh, I suppose because Mrs. Lowrey came in. It would have been a little too rough for her."

"What do you mean?" Larry asked.

"Oh, you know. Some language shouldn't be said in front of ladies."

"Well, I'm glad I'm a boy!" Larry declared.

"Oh?"

"Yeah. Then I get to hear all the wild stories."

"Well, I don't know about that, Larry. I guess if the story is too bad for ladies, it's bad for all of us."

He's right of course. Some things shouldn't be said in front of anyone.

Good moms don't hesitate to take the role of family censor. Whether it is a matter of grammar or vocabulary, good moms care what is said and how it is said—and kids usually know it.

"Don't let Mom see that magazine."

"If my mother knew I was going to a movie like this . . ."

"Knock it off—here comes Mom."

Good moms are also speech teachers. Who else teaches your children to speak correctly? Oh, they'll pick up their dialect from their cultural heritage or geographical location. They will learn some grammar from their schoolteacher. But there's much more to learning how to speak. Where do they learn the dos and don'ts about Christian speech?

Our current society doesn't hold much stock in words that are spoken. You can blurt out about anything, in any gathering, and it hardly raises an eyebrow. Words don't even have a lot of value. You have to have something in writing before you're bound.

That's not the biblical view of speech. Listen to what Jesus said in Matthew 12:36-37: "And I say to you, that every careless word that men shall speak, they shall render account for it in the day of judgment. For by your words you shall be justified, and by your words you shall be condemned."

"Every careless word" refers to useless words. Our society may demean the meaning of words, but they remain of critical importance to God. That's why moms must teach their kids how to speak well.

That's not an easy task, especially when moms still struggle with control themselves. James 3:2 states, "If anyone does not stumble in what he says, he is a perfect man, able to bridle the whole body as well." The one who can completely control his speech at all times is the perfect person. He goes on in verse 8, "But no one can tame the tongue; it is a restless evil and full of deadly poison."

No one can tame the tongue completely. It remains a wild animal that can turn vicious at any moment. However, it can be caged. It can be kept within bounds, with the Lord's help and with a mom who teaches the rules of Christian speech.

Guidelines to Teach Your Children

SPEAK THE TRUTH

"Therefore, laying aside falsehood, speak truth, each one of you, with his neighbor, for we are members of one another" (Ephesians 4:25).

No matter how much the trusting brown eyes warm our hearts, this darling child was born with a sin nature. By nature, every man, woman, boy, and girl will do and say whatever is to his best advantage, whether it be the gospel truth or a boldfaced lie.

Telling the truth is relating what really happened. It's retelling the facts as you experienced them or heard them. Truth can be embarrassing, or painful, or funny, or boring, or exciting, or sad, and the only base on which the future may be safely built. It is virtue in every legitimate, legal, moral vocation.

Kids that are trained to tell the truth have a three step head start on everyone else.

KEEP THEIR WORD

"But let your statement be, 'Yes, yes' or 'No, no'; and anything beyond these is of evil" (Matthew 5:37).

In Jesus' day the claim was made that a promise was good only if a proper vow was attached to it. It's like our saying, "I swear on a stack of Bibles that this is the truth."

Jesus taught that we should simply be able to say, "Yes, I'll do it," or, "No, I will not," and then stand by our word.

First, we need to help our children recognize when they've made a promise. "I'll take my bath right after this show's over" is a promise. It does not mean "After the show, and after I eat some ice cream, and after I play with my puzzle."

SPEAK SOUNDLY

Be "sound in speech which is beyond reproach, in order that the opponent may be put to shame, having nothing bad to say about us" (Titus 2:8).

Sound speech is speech free from defect, speech that is stable, based on reason, sensible. You wouldn't be ashamed to have anyone hear what you said.

SPEAK WITH GRACE

"Let your speech always be with grace, seasoned, as it were with salt, so that you may know how you should respond to each person" (Colossians 4:6).

Gracious speech is based on good will. It keeps the conversation on the highest level. Paul uses an interesting description here: "seasoned with salt." We think of salty language as the notorious curses of sailors on the open sea. For Paul, salt meant preservative. Salt retarded spoilage. Our language should be so couched as to keep the conversation from degenerating into the insipid, degrading, or obscene.

BE SLOW TO SPEAK

"But let everyone be quick to hear, slow to speak and slow to anger" (James 1:19).

It's simple but profound advice. Don't get in a hurry to jump into the conversation. For one thing, you may not have heard all that was said and may find yourself way off track. For another, you may blurt out words that you haven't thought through.

Those most likely to speak too quickly are those who are unsure of themselves and are feeling the necessity to impress by cleverness, humor, quick wit, or boasting. They are the very ones who need most to slow down. Challenge your children: "Did you hear what you just said?" "Did you really mean that?" "Why don't you let Sissy finish first?"

BE NOBLE IN THEIR SPEECH

"Listen, for I shall speak noble things; and the opening of my lips will produce right things" (Proverbs 8:6).

To be noble is to exhibit the highest moral qualities. To speak nobly is to let these qualities be reflected in your words and tone. "Finally, brethren, whatever is true, whatever is honorable, whatever is right, whatever is pure, whatever is lovely, whatever is of good repute, if there is any excellence and if anything worthy of praise, let your mind dwell on these things" (Philippians 4:8).

Now, at this point you may be thinking, *All of that is well and good theoretically. But what about little Junior who's in the living room with his Gotron Laser Gun threatening to blast Sissy clear to the planet Zakworth?*

Good question. The only solution is to ease into one particular conversation, one day at a time. And be thankful for every tiny bit of progress.

Aaron used to call anyone he got upset with either "meathead" or "peanut brain." Now the house rule is that he can use those names only in fun with his two big brothers, and they can return the favor. They're not names for Mom or Dad or friends.

This week we're working to eliminate the phrase "I'm going to kill you."

SPEAK ABOUT GOD WITHOUT FEAR

Paul asks the Philippians to pray for him that he might "have far more courage to speak the word of God without fear" (Philippians 1:14).

Since our society, for the most part, tends to be hostile toward God, it can be threatening even for adults to bring up spiritual subjects. We don't want to be stereotyped into a mold we don't fit. We don't want to stir up some old prejudice with a long tirade about the evils of religion. Or perhaps someone will challenge us to defend our statements and possibly expose some weakness in our knowledge and understanding. Suppose they decide that if that's the way we believe they won't have anything to do with us anymore.

Kids face similar pressures. They're not even sure it's legal to talk about God at school. The best way for them to feel at ease talking about the Lord any time, any place, is to watch how we do it.

BE A GOOD EXAMPLE

"Let no one look down on your youthfulness, but rather in speech, conduct, love, faith, and purity, show yourself an example of those who believe" (1 Timothy 4:12).

A child needs to be encouraged to be a leader, rather than always a follower. To be sure, each child has a different temperament with an introverted or extroverted tendency. But no one has to always go along with the gang.

Phil was called a "goody-goody boy" when he was eight. By junior high he was know as the "deacon" because he was the only one on the ball team who refused to cuss. He took a lot of razzing from the guys, but they should have begun to see the light when they were sophomores and all the girls voted Phil the most gentlemanly guy at Sea View High School. Still, the old gang was shocked when, at age twenty-one, the "deacon" married the undisputed beauty queen of the city.

More than a couple of guys regretted that they hadn't followed Phil's example years before.

GIVE PROPER CREDIT TO CHRIST

"For I will not presume to speak of anything except what Christ has accomplished through me" (Romans 15:18).

From the time they learn to sing and believe "Jesus loves me, this I know, for the Bible tells me so," children are able to give thanks for God's work in their lives. They shouldn't grow up thinking that only preachers, old men, and ladies with big black Bibles are supposed to tell others about God.

Kids have lots of questions about the world of the spirit. "What happens when we die?" "Why can't I see God?" "Do dogs go to heaven?" "Where was I before I was born?"

We won't have all the answers, but that's OK. They'll begin to know that there will always be some things they won't understand. But what they do know to be true, from what they experience and what they study in the Bible, they can tell others. Such as, "He helps me not be afraid," "He listens to me when I pray."

The detailed speech lessons of Scripture don't stop with exhortations on what elements should be included in our talk. They give clear direction on what should be eliminated as well. As you are teaching your children what they should say, remind them what they should not say as well.

TENDENCIES TO DISCOURAGE IN YOUR CHILDREN

ABUSIVE SPEECH

Put aside "abusive speech from your mouth" (Colossians 3:8). Abusive speech insults, mistreats, or harms. Words are the most deadly tools children are freely allowed to play with. We are shocked when parents leave guns or knives in easy access around the house, but many more lives have been crippled and ruined by words.

FILTHY SPEECH

"There must be no filthiness" (Ephesians 5:4).

Different cultures might define filthy talk in different ways. It's fairly well defined in our society. These are the arsenal of words that describe body parts, body functions, and sexual relationships.

THE USE OF DRIVEL

"There must be no . . . silly talk" (Ephesians 5:4). Kids are silly. They like having fun. The Bible's not against that. The intent that Paul has in mind here refers to the habit of droning on with trivial words that have no meaning and accomplish no purpose. This is particularly bad when the occasion requires reverence or an attitude of seriousness. There are times to be silent or refrain from incessant banter.

DISRESPECTFUL JOKES

"There must be no . . . coarse jesting" (Ephesians 5:4). This does not just mean dirty stories, but they are included. And it does not just mean bigoted ethnic jokes, but they're certainly part of it. We should avoid all speech with veiled implications and distasteful double meanings.

THE USE OF FLATTERY AS A WEAPON

"For we never came with flattering speech" (1 Thessalonians 2:5). There is a great difference between a compliment and flattery. A compliment is a word or act of praise acknowledging something that was done well. Seldom do we compliment a person too often.

Flattery, on the other hand, is used to glorify insincerely by making something appear to be even more attractive than it is. Flattery aims for areas in which a person has little or no control, such as "You have the most beautiful brown eyes in the world." That does not acknowledge achievement, but rather appeals to vanity in order to gain some advantage.

SPEAKING DISRESPECTFULLY OF MOTHER OR FATHER

"For God said, 'Honor your father and mother' " (Matthew 15:4). Jesus quoted one of the Ten Commandments, of course. To honor implies not to speak evil of. We seem to be losing our esteem for this command.

No parent is perfect (not even parents who write books on how to be good moms and dads). And some parents do little to encourage the respect of their children. However, a principle is at work here. The role of a parent places him in a position worthy of honor. In a two parent home, one parent can work to guard the honor of the other. In single parent homes where the guardian parent is being dishonored, perhaps an outside mediator or counselor can provide support for curbing the destructive habit of putting down Mom or Dad.

TOPICS THAT ARE TABOO

"For it is disgraceful even to speak of the things which are done by them in secret" (Ephesians 5:12). What would you consider an off-limits subject in your household? What would you say or do if such a thing was mentioned?

PUT DOWNS OF FAMILY MEMBERS

"Do not speak against one another, brethren" (James 4:11). Junior does not have weird ears, Sissy is not a slimeball, Robert is not stupid, and Candy does not have bowling pin legs. Until the apologies come, there's no television, no stereo, and no dessert.

THE ABUSE OF GOD'S NAME

"You shall not take the name of the Lord your God in vain" (Exodus 20:7). God's name is holy because He is holy. One day every human who ever lived will bow down before the name of Jesus Christ. Those who toss His name around lightly will face unbearable shame in that moment.

Does this task seem overwhelming? It will if our goal is to make our children accountable for every syllable and phrase that come out of their mouths. That would be oppressive for them and for us. Remember the last time you blurted out something you deeply regretted? We sure do. Only in a spirit of love and forgiveness and renewed humility can you pick yourself up and go on with God's next step for you. That's the experience we need to remember as we correct our children.

Here are some guidelines that have helped us in this task:

Work with one goal at a time. Help them understand and apply one standard before moving on to another. A long list can seem impossible.

Use encouraging words to correct them. Using abusive speech to correct abusive speech will never accomplish anything. The trick is to point out a better speech alternative, without putting them down in the process.

Exhibit correct speech yourself. Let them know what you need to work on. Correct yourself in public and apologize. Show them how a person can get back on track.

Allow them to correct you. Let them know that you are following the same standards you expect from them. Encourage your husband to do the same.

Richard Halverson, chaplain of the United States Senate, has recorded this prayer for those "word merchants" in the chamber: "Lord, help them to appreciate the power of words . . . to honor, to disparage; to encourage, to disappoint; to comfort, to embarrass; to edify, to offend; to strengthen, to weaken; to motivate, to immobilize; to give hope, to frustrate; to purify, to pollute; to build, and to destroy."

Kids are going to learn to talk. And their words will have power. May we pray for and teach the "word merchants" under our care.

8

Mom Baked a Cake,
and My Name's on Top!

"Teddy J. Simpson, you're one great kid." Mary Lou and Renie giggled as they raced out of the Junior High gym.

"What's that all about?" Shawn asked Teddy as they stood in line to finish another basketball practice drill.

"Oh, you know, just seventh graders—" Teddy replied as coolly as he could. But he wondered himself.

As Teddy bounced his basketball home, Darrell Myers rode by on his bike shouting, "Hey, Teddy J. Simpson, you're one great kid!" and then sped on down the street toward the library.

Teddy was shaking his head and mumbling to himself as he rounded the corner and headed up the hill to his house. Then he stopped dead in his tracks.

There, draped across the entire garage door of the Simpson house, was a six-by-twenty-foot banner that proclaimed to all passersby: TEDDY J. SIMPSON, YOU ARE ONE GREAT KID!

"Oh, no," he groaned, "what's my mother up to now?"

He dashed into the house. The dining room table was set with the best dishes, and the famous red plate, used for special events like birthdays and anniversaries, was at the head of the table. "There's even cloth napkins!" Teddy mumbled. "We never have cloth napkins unless Grandma is coming over."

In the kitchen Teddy's mom casually peeled potatoes.

Teddy began in staccato. "What's happening? What's the sign for? Are we having company for dinner? Who's the red plate for? How come nobody ever tells me anything?"

"Whoa," his mother interrupted. "What sign are you talking about?"

"What sign? What sign? The six-foot-high 'Teddy J. Simpson, you're one great kid' sign. That's what sign."

"Oh, yes. Well" —his mother smiled— "I just figured that the kid who won 'Best of the Fair' grand prize at the city-wide Science Fair ought to be congratulated in a proper manner. We're having a party."

"What?"

"A party."

"No, no, no. I mean, I won Best of the Fair? Are you kidding? A high schooler always wins that."

"Not this year. I got a call from the superintendent of sc. ools. They are very proud of your project. They will want to get a picture of you for the paper. I would have told you sooner, but you were staying late for basketball practice."

The next day at school Shawn questioned him about the sign.

"Was it because of the science project?"

"Oh, you know, moms are crazy sometimes."

Shawn nodded. "Yeah, your mom's something else,"

"Yeah, I know," Teddy J. Simpson said as he walked a little taller into his first period class.

Most of the events you remember from childhood will be those that were attached to the biggest celebrations. Do you remember your tenth birthday party? Your eleventh? Probably not. They're dusty relics locked in a mental storage vault labeled "olden days."

Do you remember your twelfth birthday party? Good chance. That may have been the time Mom allowed you to have that slumber party. You invited as many friends as your parents allowed. You all got to sleep down in the den, had pizza delivered from Momma Maria's, and stayed up until 4:00 A.M. playing Elvis Presley or

Beatles records. In the first twenty years of your life that night has to go down as one of the top ten.

Some things in life are worth celebrating. Sometimes just plain living is worth celebrating.

God's people have always known how to celebrate great events. They danced and sang when God led them out of Egypt (Exodus 5:1) and promised God they would keep celebrating every year from then on (Exodus 12:14). In fact, they made a covenant to establish three annual celebrations (Exodus 23:14).

Also, they commemorated the building of the Temple (1 Kings 8) and the rebuilding of the Temple hundreds of years later (Ezra 6:16). And those were just the national celebrations.

Jesus began His miracle working ministry at a wedding party (John 2:1-11). He promised things like "abundant life" (John 10:10) and "joy . . . made full" (John 15:11). More than any other group of people on the face of the earth, Christians of every culture, every economic strata, every dialect have the truest motivation to celebrate all the good things God brings to them.

Party mom. It sounds like a reckless, irresponsible parent. In this case it stands for a mom who tries to break out of some family ruts once in a while. Let's take a look at some traditional—and not so traditional—times where moms can be the grand family hostess.

REASONS TO CELEBRATE

BIRTHDAYS

Birthdays are the easiest to remember but so common you might feel tapped out of creativity. Here's why you need to try anyway.

No one in the family gets overlooked. Sissy's senior year will be filled with memories, while Junior gets shoved to the side—except on his birthday. The prima donna senior is just one of the guests on that day. Junior is the center of attention.

Birthday bashes are good for building sibling unity. "Yes, you do have to buy Todd a present, even if he spilled your best perfume and called your new boyfriend a nerd."

It's a great time to share thanks to God. After all, it was His idea that this particular person become a member of this family. Birthdays help focus on that one family member rather than always lumping him as part of the group.

Here are five birthday ideas:

- Invite as many friends as the age of the birthday child.
- Have guests bring inexpensive gifts in multiples of the birthday year. (For example: twelve dimes, twelve pencils with her name on them, twelve stamps, and so on.)
- Ask your child where she would celebrate her birthday if she could go anywhere in the world. Then transform your dining room, and the corresponding menu, to match. (Hawaiian shirts, dark glasses, travel posters, hula music, roast pork, and baked pineapple, or whatever.)
- Months ahead of time, ask your child who, of all the famous people in the world, he would most like to invite to his birthday party. Then, invite those on his list. You can find addresses for political figures and TV stars if you look hard enough. No, of course they won't come, but many will send at least a form letter acknowledgment.
- Start the day after this year's birthday. Secretly clip, save, or note down the most dramatic things that happen to your child each week. You should end up with about fifty-two events to plaster in a scrapbook and present as "This Was the Year That Was."

HOLIDAYS

Why make them important?

Our forefathers set aside these special days for a good reason. They should mean more to us than just a three-day weekend.

Holidays help unify our communities and our country. It's not by accident that God has selected you for this time and place.

Holidays emphasize cultural and political values that are worthy to be handed down from one generation to the next, and such celebrations are good opportunities to do just that.

Here are some guidelines for national holiday celebrations.

- Some are worth a big celebration every year (i.e., Independence Day), while others might rotate in their significance for the family (Columbus Day, President's Day, and so on).
- Think of a particular family activity that is to be associated with that particular holiday. (On the Fourth of July Mom reads the Declaration of Independence, on Memorial Day we drive out to the cemetery and place flowers on Grandpa's grave, on Thanksgiving Day we make a list of things we are thankful for and spend time together in prayer, and so on.)
- Whenever possible, aim for joining into any community event scheduled for that day. Teach your children respect and pride for the achievements of the past.

ANNIVERSARIES

- Celebrate the years you've lived in your present house. (Does five years seem like no big deal? It will be if your kids spent their first ten years in twelve different locations.)
- Celebrate the number of years Dad's been on the job. ("It's his tenth year of teaching!")
- Celebrate the first anniversary of Sissy's driver's license—one year without a traffic ticket.
- Celebrate the anniversary of Junior's skateboard championship.
- Celebrate the anniversary of Lisa's learning how to ride a horse.
- And, by all means, celebrate your wedding anniversary. (More about that in chapter 13.)

VICTORIES

Victories come in all sizes. Some are known by the whole community. Some are never heard of outside the walls of your house. Victories signify achievement. Achievement means hard work. Victories also imply the possibility of loss or defeat. No victory was ever won without a risk. Celebrate when:

- Junior quits sucking his thumb
- Dad gets the promotion
- Sissy makes the drill team

- Lisa loses ten pounds (a low-cal party, please!)
- Robert finally passes algebra
- You finish the quilt for Grandma (after it spent ten years in the closet)
- Junior makes it home without getting mud on his new coat (hey, take any victory you can)
- Sissy gets the lead in the school play
- You get an "A" in your night school psychology class

NO GOOD REASON AT ALL

Start with an off-the-wall whim—no special date, no anniversary, no achievement—just party-time. When do you do such a thing?

- When somebody was really counting on winning, and they lost
- Half-way between last year's vacation and next year's
- After a week and a half of being cooped in the house because the weather's been too bad to go outside
- When it's the end of the month, and you can't afford to take everyone out to dinner
- When you get your tax estimates and find out you still owe $4,000 (plan a garage sale at the party)
- When everybody is going to Christine's party, but Sissy has chicken pox
- When today has been about the most boring day you've ever experienced

You get the idea. Off-the-wall, spur of the moment parties could be your best. That's when you can use up all those odds and ends of paper goods and party stuff. You don't have to follow any color theme. You don't even have to tell them what the party's all about. Let them guess. Sort of a "name that party."

MAKE THEM SPECIAL

Make them public whenever possible. Put a poster on the apartment bulletin board; drive a handpainted sign in the front lawn; run a little ad in the local paper.

Make them family sponsored. Give every family member a job to do in preparing for the celebration. It's not something that Mom does alone, but a statement by the whole gang.

Make them fun. Use an old pair of tennies painted fire-engine red and mounted on a board to celebrate Dad's completion of the company 10-K run (signifying that he burned up the course, naturally).

CELEBRATE THE THINGS GOD HAS DONE

It is critical for building strong faith in your kids for them to remember plainly how God has worked in the past. We can so easily forget even the most significant events. Could the people of Israel ever forget how God led them en masse out of Egypt, took care of them personally for forty years, and then brought them into the Promised Land? Sure. So God appointed them a yearly celebration called Passover. That should keep their eye on God at least once a year, right? Nope. After a while they even forgot to celebrate Passover. It was King Josiah (in 2 Chronicles 35) who reinstituted the celebration.

We must work hard not to forget what God has done. Celebrate the things He has done for all of us.

- Christmas—when Immanuel, "God in the flesh," came to dwell among us
- Good Friday—when Jesus died for our sins
- Easter—when Christ rose from the dead proving that we will be able to live forever with Him
- Pentecost—the birthday of the church

The world can commercialize them or ignore them, but for those of us who believe in Christ, these are the big celebrations of our year. There are some things in life worth getting out the good dishes, baking a cake, giving a gift, and shouting Hallelujah over.

Personal family celebrations are needed as well.

- to rejoice over Junior's confession of faith and baptism
- to honor Sissy's first solo in church
- to thank the Lord for the doctor's report on Dad

- to praise God for providing the new house
- to celebrate the whole family's memorizing Psalm 23

For those who think being a party mom sounds intimidating or tiring or both, the good news is you don't have to try all these ideas in the same week or the same month or the same year. Just try one, and see what happens.

You'll build memories—good memories. That's a sound foundation for whatever lies ahead for you and your children.

You'll establish a unique family history, a past, a tradition. Your children will know that they are somebodies.

You'll be setting an example for your children when they become parents of their own 2.4 children or whatever the average will be by then.

You'll emphasize a focus on the good experiences of growing up interspersed with the tough times. It helps keep the perspective of life on this earth in balance.

You'll be preserving family unity with this common shared background, which means doing your part to preserve a God-given institution. All celebrations that stay within biblical guidelines, no matter what the reason for their existence, are really statements of praise to God. We're letting Him know that, indeed, He has been very good to us, and we're tasting a part of the abundant life.

So go for it. Be a party mom.

9

Where's Aunt Martha's
Oldest Boy Now?

In the spring of 1873 Steve's maternal great-great grandfather, W. E. Hall, moved his whole tribe from Decatur, Alabama, to Bosque County, Texas. They settled down on a place not too far from where the Chisholm Trail crossed the Brazos River.

That's just a little bit of trivia out of our family history. It may have no significance for you, but it's very fascinating to us. But we had no knowledge of that information until January of 1987 when we received a phone call from a distant relative in Decatur, Alabama, who was doing research on the family.

Most of us knew that Steve's Granny Wilson was born and raised in Texas, but she had never told the California kin about the sojourns in Alabama. So how did these folks find us? Well, it seems a great aunt's daughter in Texas knew a second cousin in Oklahoma, and she remembered that Aunt Katie had gone to California years ago and had two daughters.

Moms can remember relatives better than anyone else in the world.

Much of the Bible is the story of remembering families. Each of our family trees trace back one way or another to that Garden of Eden. Then God picked out one family, Abraham's, and chose to make them His instrument of blessing for the world. Many genera-tions down the line, descendants continued to refer to those very dis-tant relatives as "Abraham, Isaac, and Jacob, our forefathers."

What do Hezron, Abiud, Joram, Matthan, Hesli, Cosam, and Reu all have in common? They were all far-flung relations of Jesus. Read through Matthew 1 or Luke 4, and you'll find dozens of these folks mentioned. Where did Matthew and Luke get their lists? No one had written about them for hundreds of years. Their names were passed down orally, from family to family. By the time Matthew and Luke began to write, Jesus had returned to heaven. Joseph, earthly father of Jesus, is never mentioned during Jesus' ministry, so it is as-sumed he had already died. But Mary was very much alive.

Mary was at the cross when Jesus died. She is recorded in atten-dance at the beginning of the church (Acts 1). At least one of the genealogies may have come from Mary herself. After all, it's the kind of thing a mother remembers.

THE FACTS ABOUT FAMILIES

If you're like the typical family of today, we can probably assume a few basic things.

YOUR KIDS AREN'T INTERESTED

Your kids probably won't be interested in your family history until it's too late. To our Aaron, seven at this writing, the "olden days" are anything prior to 1980. He doesn't even like us to talk about any-thing that we did as a family before he was around.

While they were in their teens, our older sons centered their worlds on the most immediate events. Talking about the past harked too close to a history lecture or classroom assignment. Now their at-tentions are geared to establishing homes and careers. But once the babies start coming, it will begin to hit them. The kids are growing up, and they never got to go ocean fishing with this great-grandpa or backpacking with that uncle. In fact, they will never even know them.

One day vague memories of tales will float back to them. Didn't Grandpa say he traveled overland from Indian Territory out to California? What about that horse ranch back in Illinois? Then somewhere around age thirty-five or forty they'll hanker to sit down with the old gentleman and pick his brain with a hundred questions. But he'll be gone.

However, if a mom, somewhere down the line, has gathered a written collection of those stories and names and dates, they're not lost forever. They remain for a new age of kids.

If your kids are going to hear the important lessons from another generation you will probably have to initiate the conversation.

If the elder folks of your family are still around, don't wait for your children to ask them all the right questions or for the elders to initiate the stories of the past. You may need to be a mediator.

"Granny, tell Sissy about the first date you had with Gramps. Where did you go? What did you wear? How did you comb your hair? Were you nervous?"

"Uncle Matt, tell Junior about that time you sailed off to Australia to prospect for opals and got lost in the Indian Ocean."

"Mom, tell the kids about that first Thanksgiving you and Dad had during the Depression, the one in which you lived in that two-room flat above the Turkish bakery in Pittsburgh."

"Grandpa, tell us all you can remember about *your* grandpa."

Even better, how fortunate is the family who has elder members who write memories in a diary, journal, or scrapbook of some kind.

Your kids will likely not always want to go visit relatives, but you should make them go anyway.

Taking a trip to a relative's, especially ones they know little or not at all, may place low on your child's "Things I Want to Do" list. Watching the fourteenth rerun of a Disney cartoon may rate considerably higher.

However, such a paltry excuse would not keep them out of school, for instance. And this can be a very educational experience for them, as well as surprisingly pleasant.

Not all of our kin will have fascinating stories to share, but they can all teach lessons in building a family history that shapes where they've come from.

YOU WILL HAVE DIFFERENCES

Some of your relatives will have life-styles with which you don't agree.

The guy your sister's living with now is the third one since last Christmas. When they visit you Junior keeps asking, "Where's Uncle Chip?" "Where's Uncle Mel?"

Then there's your husband's brother Max who rides with a motorcycle gang, has a beard down to his belt buckle, and displays on his right arm a two-color tattoo of a hula dancer.

Both your sister and your husband's brother have invited your kids to come spend a few days with them. So far, you've always had some good excuse.

Don't disown the relatives, but also don't lower your standards. It might be, for the time being, that your close communication with these family members should be mainly by letter, card, or phone call. Closer contact may not result in the kind of education you've been looking for.

Some of your relatives will be real characters.

Great Uncle Clarence is a bachelor who still lives on the family farm outside of Springfield. At night he sits beside a round-top radio and listens to the livestock report from Chicago. Piled behind his barn is every piece of farm equipment ever used on the old place for the past 120 years. He's got a story for every one of them. Each Christmas for the past thirty that you can remember he has sent two pint jars of homemade blackberry preserves. Your kids have just got to meet Uncle Clarence.

Then there's cousin Ben, who was an engineer on a train, went back to school to become an architect, lived in Kenya designing government buildings, and now teaches African history at the University. You've got to get the gang back to New England to see Ben. His model train collection alone would be worth the trip.

Some might border on the famous, some might border on the bizarre, but they are all yours.

Your family will respond to some relatives better than to others.
It's only natural. Some of them have children closer to your kids'
ages. Some will live down the street instead of twelve hundred miles
away. Some will like camping as does your family.

Even when visiting distant relatives, some your gang will feel instantly at home, and others will be a real strain.

No problem. All of them are equally related, and you are going to
keep that idea before your family. But some do produce a special
bond, and you are just going to spend more time and effort on those
relationships.

You cannot get close to every relative. Those with whom you will
become really close are limited in the same way your close friends are
limited. At an intimate level you can only stretch yourself so far.

That doesn't mean you can't enjoy them all. Some you will see every week, and some every month, and some every year, and some
you never see but will remember just the same.

YOU WILL HAVE TO TAKE THE INITIATIVE

*Some of your relatives will have separated themselves from you on
purpose.*

Perhaps an event from the past, either a conflict, misunderstand-
ing, or just plain neglect has pulled you away from a segment of your
roots. Mothers can many times prevent this distance from becoming
too vast for the next generation. If possible, work to heal the hurt,
arbitrate the differences, or understand their position.

Don't assume that because they have separated themselves from
some family members they want to be removed from you as well.
Your Aunt Nellie might not be speaking to your father, but she just
might want to hear from you.

Also, don't assume that the situation is unchangeable. Attempt to
open up a line of communication. When Junior asks, "Why don't
Aunt Nellie and Gramps ever talk to each other?" it's pretty hard to
explain.

Some of your relatives will seem to get lost, no matter how hard you try to find them.

Relatives disappear. Your brother's oldest daughter married a drummer in a country western band, and no one has heard from her in about seven years.

Don't give up the search. Keep asking about them. Keep praying for them. Sooner or later everybody needs a family. Someday the niece who married the drummer may want to look up the aunt who's been asking about her for years.

Some of your relatives will never seem to initiate any contact with you.

Your husband's sister, Shirley, never writes unless you write first. Her Christmas card always arrives one week after you've sent one to her, and she never includes a note, just signs her name. She seems pleasant enough when you stop by for a visit, but in fifteen years she's never once come to visit you. When you question your husband, he just says, "Oh, that's the way Shirl is."

As discouraging as it may be, you'll have to carry the load and keep initiating the friendship. Some folks just aren't very good at it. Some are so entrapped with their own family predicaments or interests that they can't seem to reach out any further. But that doesn't necessarily mean they don't enjoy cards, pictures, and visits from you.

If you don't keep the lines open to the larger family unit it probably just won't get done.

Your husband may call his mother every month or so and talk to his sister and brother once or twice a year. That's it. Without you, the family will drift into isolationism and lose much in the way of its heritage, tradition, and adventure.

It's a big responsibility for moms. But you do it.

You do it because good relationships are worth keeping. You do it because you know all people are special and important. You do it because it's the right thing to do. You do it because you're the mom.

How can you possibly keep up with such a big task? Here are a dozen suggestions that might give you some inspiration.

IDEAS FOR KEEPING FAMILY TIES STRONG

MAKE AND MAINTAIN A LITERAL FAMILY TREE

Don't just talk about the old family tree. Make one.

Take the inside of a closet door and make it the official location of the family tree. Buy some poster board, or just stretch butcher paper the full length of the door. (Double thick so the markers won't bleed through.) Fasten it securely. Then start the tree. Leave some room at the bottom for your children's spouses and children. (Yes, it will happen someday.) Start with you and your husband. List your full names, birthdates, and the cities and states in which you were born. Draw lines down to your children below, add the parents of each of you above, and then push it on up as far as you can go.

Write small. You probably have a lot more to fill in that you would think. Keep all the same generation on the same horizontal line.

Now when they get a birthday card from your Aunt Ida in Des Moines, go to the chart and show them how she is related.

One of our friends embroidered and framed a plaque bearing this data for her living room wall. Another friend found an old sampler folded in a hundred-year-old family Bible with family names she hadn't known existed. She carefully framed this treasure behind glass.

ENCOURAGE LETTER WRITING BY ALL FAMILY MEMBERS

Maybe the most efficient way to do this is to pre-address envelopes (postcards, if the kids are young). Have the stamps already in place. Then, at dinner time, or some similar get-together, place a letter or card and pen at each plate and have them jot a note off before they leave the table.

Teach them that good letters don't have to be profound, just personal. Encourage them to ask one question in each letter. That will give the recipient a good reason to write back and continue to build the relationship. The younger they are when they begin to correspond, the more likely you will be able to build a habit that lasts.

The most natural and appreciated time to have your children write is when acknowledging a gift. We always treasure the thank-yous and other notes we receive from nieces and nephews and other young people. In fact, we have quite a file of correspondence from various family members we felt were significant enough to keep (sometimes just because we so rarely hear from them). We make sure to add the date, if it's not on the letter.

HOLD AN ANNUAL FAMILY GATHERING

It might be the proverbial family picnic. Or it could be a Fourth of July gathering at Granny's. Or Thanksgiving up at the lake.

If no such event is happening, then consider staging it yourself. Invite all known relatives and have a party. Even if your family unit is small right now, it will grow. And as it grows it will have a grand tradition of yearly celebrations to hang onto.

Have everyone bring the food. Share the cost of renting the gazebo at the park. Toss in some balls and games for the kids, plenty of lawn chairs for the old folks, then go have some fun.

READ LETTERS FROM FAMILY MEMBERS ALOUD

Kids and husbands are notorious for never reading everything in a letter from Grandma. And does your husband *ever* read a letter from your sister?

Again, family mealtime might be just the place. Read the whole letter. Stop when different family members are mentioned and check to see that they know who you are talking about. It might be a trip to the old family tree is needed to clarify the matter.

They might not say much at the time, but the information is being stored up for future reference.

HAVE EACH CHILD "ADOPT" A DIFFERENT OLDER RELATIVE

Grandmas and Grandpas don't count here—they belong to everyone. Have them choose a more distant relative (like Grandma's sister).

This one can be their special pen pal. They get extra cards, homemade pictures, and surprises. They get photocopies of newspaper pictures of Junior on his dirt bike.

They always get a class picture and a little gift at Christmas. The impact that such concern of a little one for this senior citizen will not be able to be measured this side of heaven. Don't be surprised to get a phone call now and then from Uncle Harry in Florida, who wants only to talk to "my little Sissy."

HAVE FAMILY CHRISTMAS PHOTOS TAKEN

It doesn't have to be an expensive portrait setting. Use the supermarket holiday coupons and get down for a picture. These don't have to be sent to all your friends. They are to be sent to all the relatives you can afford to send to. Besides your holiday greetings, turn the photo over, take a felt tip pen (so as to not damage the photo), and label it. Write on the back of the photo itself, not on the cute little holiday filler to the side. Write the current date, the full name of all the kids and their ages.

Sure Uncle Harry knows you by sight, and you haven't changed a bit since last year. But Uncle Harry is going to cut off the holiday greeting and put that treasure in his scrapbook. Then twenty-five years from now Harry's granddaughter, Tina, will dust off the old books as she sits in her North Carolina beachfront home, and she'll stare for a moment at that grinning gang. She'll pull out the photo, look on the back, and recognize your name. For just a moment she'll remember the one time she met you at her Grandpa Harry's funeral. She'll remember how she and Sissy were the two that did the most crying, and how warm and sincere your hug felt afterward. And as she sips her coffee and stares at the photo a tear will roll down her cheek. Suddenly life is not quite so lonely as she had thought only a few moments before.

That sixty seconds spent labeling a Christmas photo made her day.

GET YOUR PHOTOS LABELED AND IN AN ALBUM

How many years have you been saying, "Someday I'll get those all organized"? If a photo isn't safely secured and properly labeled it's hardly worth keeping. An unknown picture is not worth a thousand words; it's worthless.

Again, with a felt tip pen, label the back of the photos with names (so that a stranger could identify them, for example, "Granny in the purple hat—") and date of the photo. Also add the place where the picture was taken, and the occasion, if you can remember it.

You aren't recording trivial statistics, you're recording history. Make it accurate.

Once you get caught up, the procedure is simpler. Label and mount the pictures as soon as you get them. Week by week there aren't all that many. It's year by year, and decade by decade, that they start to pile up.

We have a habit in our house of designating one full wall for family photos. It's like a Bly gallery. As we find new photos we want to display, we either expand the wall, or replace some of the old ones. One feature is a blown up photo from each family vacation. The most prominent right now is a poster sized setting of Janet with Russell and Mike standing at Bowman Lake in Glacier National Park. It's decoupaged onto a table top that Russell made in a shop class.

MOUNT A MAP OF THE U.S. OR WORLD

Place a map on an accessible wall in the house so that you can locate your whole tribe geographically. Place red marks or pins on the towns in which your relatives live. When you get a letter from a distant state, remind everyone of where Odessa, Texas, is. The map is also an excellent place to go to follow Grandma's trip to the East Coast and Cousin Rusty's bike ride from Mexico to Canada.

SHARE SPIRITUAL EVENTS WITH YOUR RELATIVES

If the event is important to you, tell your family about it, even if they don't seem interested in spiritual things. Tell them about Junior's conversion at camp. Tell them about your husband's selection as a deacon. Tell them of how the Lord answered your prayers about Sissy's illness. Tell them about the dynamic missions speaker that convinced your whole family to spend three weeks rebuilding an orphanage in Mexico this summer.

You don't have to be a preacher or evangelist. But make sure they know how important Jesus Christ is in your life, and how He is constantly working to help guide your family .

PRAY FOR YOUR RELATIVES AS A FAMILY

If you prayed for each family just once a week that would be fifty-two families per year. That should include almost everyone.

A set of three-by-five cards with names, kids, and ages is all that is needed. Draw one card every Sunday lunch (or whenever), and pray for them. Perhaps you will know them and their needs very well, perhaps you will lack specific knowledge about them, but pray anyway.

Some years we have done this with our Christmas cards. We place them in a basket and draw one out every day or so. Some friends of ours told us they write follow-up notes to tell particular relatives that they're being prayed for.

One final project just for you moms. Since you're the unofficial designated protector of the family heritage and tradition, keep a regular family diary.

"Oh, but nothing much ever happens to us," you say. That's probably just what your great-great-grandmother said as she rode that rattle-banging, side-splitting old covered wagon West. But even if she had stayed East, wouldn't you love to have a journal of her life and thoughts? Just hearing about her everyday routine would be fascinating now. You can provide that thrill for your own great-grandchildren.

10

Nobody Gets Seconds Until
He Says His Memory Verse

Two dozen four- to seven-year-olds sat on the steps of the platform in front of the sanctuary as the pastor asked them, "As far as the spiritual things we do, such as prayer, study, Bible reading, going to church and all that, what does a daddy do? And what does a mommy do?"

"Daddies read the Bible at dinnertime."

"Daddies collect the money at church."

"Daddies serve the Lord's Supper."

"Daddies sort of preach sermons at home."

"Daddies paint the church."

"Daddies pray."

"What about mommies? What do they do?" the pastor urged.

"Mommies make you learn your memory verse."

"Mommies drive you to children's choir practice."

"Mommies make your costumes for the Christmas play."

"Mommies clean up after Communion."

"Mommies sing church songs at home."

"Mommies pray."

"Ah," said the pleased pastor, "both mommies and daddies pray, right?"

One very knowledgeable seven-year-old girl answered, "Yeah, both mommies and daddies pray, but there's a difference."

"What's that?"

"Well, daddies sort of—well, you feel like they're praying at you. And mommies, they pray right to God."

They pray "at" you or "with" you—a very perceptive observation for a seven-year-old.

It's not really a question of right or wrong; it's more the fact of complementary spiritual roles within the family unit. Dads and moms influence their children's spiritual growth from divergent perspectives. Yet both roles are critical.

As recorded in Acts 13, the church at Antioch had grown to the stage that they required at least five pastors (v. 1). They were about to send out the very first two official Christian missionaries, and they were uncertain of how to go about it. God helped them by speaking to them directly through the Holy Spirit. He didn't ask for volunteers. He specifically appointed Barnabas and Saul (Paul).

It was a good choice. The success of their ministry is well documented in the book of Acts. And yet, they were two very different individuals.

Paul was the preacher, teacher, and persuader. A few days after his conversion he was in the synagogue preaching about Jesus (Acts 9:20). He caused quite an uproar (vv. 21-25). That was his style. He spent the next twenty to thirty years of his life confronting people with the gospel message. This one man's boldness and persistence was a prime cause for the spread of the gospel in the first century, and the doctrine expounded in his many letters explains the Christian faith for all times and all people.

Barnabas, on the other hand, was an encourager supreme. His real name was Joseph of Cyprus, but the believers gave him the nickname Barnabas, which means "son of encouragement." In addition, he was a generous contributor to the cause of Christ. In Acts 4:36-37, we read that after his conversion he sold a large amount of land and gave not just a tithe to the apostles, but the entire sum. In a growing church (from 120 to more than 3,120 members in a matter of days), this gift was greatly appreciated and stimulated many others to give too.

Some time later, after his dramatic conversion on the Damascus road, Paul returned to Jerusalem to join with the other followers of Jesus. But he still had a reputation for arresting and jailing Christians. Could he be trusted? Was his story just a cruel ruse to gain information about the believers? They didn't want to take any chances. All but one, that is.

"But Barnabas took hold of him and brought him to the apostles and described to them how he had seen the Lord on the road, and that He had talked to him, and how at Damascus he had spoken out boldly in the name of Jesus" (Acts 9:27).

After that, Paul was accepted into fellowship. It was Barnabas who got him in.

A few years later when the church in Antioch was just beginning, the apostles sent Barnabas up to check on things. He arrived to find many new converts. It says he "rejoiced and began to encourage them all with resolute heart to remain true to the Lord" (Acts 11:23). Barnabas, always the encourager.

But he knew they needed more than just encouragement. They needed a solid teacher, too, and he knew just the man.

"And he left for Tarsus to look for Saul [Paul]; and when he had found him, he brought him to Antioch. And it came about that for an entire year they met with the church and taught considerable numbers; and the disciples were first called Christians in Antioch" (Acts 11:25-26).

Paul, the teacher, and Barnabas, the encourager . . . a great ministry team combination for the early church. Moms and dads need to work together in that way for the family's benefit too. They need a teacher and an encourager. Every family should have both.

How can you, as mom, renew your efforts at being an encourager? Maybe the following will give you some ideas.

How to Encourage Your Kids Spiritually

TEACH THEM TO WORSHIP

There is a fallacy that runs through many churches. It goes like this. If you take your kids to church regularly and deposit them in the middle of the sanctuary, they will, by some spiritual osmosis, learn to worship God. This theory is akin to tossing your children in the middle of a lake in order to teach them to swim. Some will learn to swim, some will drown, and some might make it to land but pledge never to go near the water again.

Encourage your children to read the church bulletin. Help them find the songs and urge them to follow the words (and notes) to sing. Tell them why the church takes an offering, and encourage them to give. Explain the importance of reading the Bible together.

Teach them how to listen to a sermon. Give them a pad of paper and crayons in order to draw a picture of what they hear. They could write one complete sentence of what they thought the preacher was talking about. Have them remember one story to retell later at lunch or express one thing they're going to do this week because of what they heard.

Help them to see the importance of sitting as still as possible so others won't be distracted from their worship. Tell them of how it pleases God to have His people come together and offer up a big roomful of praise.

TREAT EACH OF THEM AS INDIVIDUALS

Each will respond to a particular Bible passage or to church in general or to your spiritual nudges, in his own way. They may not all want to sing in the children's choir (though it's nice for you to have them all go together) or go to wilderness camp or visit the rest home.

Sissy may have accepted Christ as her Savior at age five, but Junior seems either unresponsive or uncomprehending at the same age. Sissy may have memorized 1 Corinthians 13, the books of the Bible, and the Ten Commandments when she was ten, but Lisa is still stuck on John 3:16 when she hits high school. They can be encouraged, but not pushed. They each walk at their own spiritual pace.

PROVIDE THEM WITH VARIED SPIRITUAL OPPORTUNITIES

We cannot make our children become Christians or exhibit spiritual growth, but we can provide them with a multitude of opportunities to do so.

At every age they could have some mandatory activities and some optional ones as well. For instance, when a child balks, insist that he go to church and participate in family devotions or prayers, but let him choose among such opportunities as camp, socials, special trips, projects, clubs, and other meetings associated with the church. Give options on a few things, even at an early age. But keep providing the reminder, the money, the transportation needed for your children to be involved in as many spiritual activities as they desire.

ENCOURAGE THEM TO TAKE THEIR SPIRITUAL EDUCATION SERIOUSLY

Any excuse that is too feeble to keep them out of public school on Monday is too feeble to keep them away from Sunday school on Sunday. We often say, "After all, you've got school tomorrow," when they plead to stay up on week nights. Do the same on Saturday nights.

If they have homework, and bring home notes from the teacher, we read the notes and see that they get the work done. Should we do any less for their Sunday school lessons?

We'll visit their school classroom for open house or to attend parent conferences. Why not show as much interest in their progress in the Sunday school? If we don't, our children pick up the message loud and clear, "Regular school is important, but what I learn at church really isn't."

JOIN IN THE LEARNING PROCESS

Learn their memory verses with them. If you have six kids, you may not have time to learn all six, but you can pick one of your own so that while they are reciting theirs, Mom can say hers as well.

Volunteer to go with their class to that special Holy Land exhibit. Think through the story about sharing that you read to your preschooler. What's the Lord trying to teach you through that story?

They may ask, "What are we going to look like in heaven?" If you don't know, tell them so, then spend some time in study to find an answer for them. Not only will you both gain some knowledge, but you'll be demonstrating to your child that when we don't know something we can study God's Book to find the answer.

MAKE LEARNING FUN

One mom takes a large newspaper ad from her children's favorite fast food restaurant. She cuts it up like a jigsaw puzzle, then each time they attend Sunday school, church, read their Bibles, or complete special projects, she glues another piece of the picture on poster board. When the picture's complete, they all go out to dinner to you know where.

Think of your own project that will prod them on but won't keep them in competition against each other. Individual achievement should receive an individual reward.

PUT THEM AT EASE ABOUT SPIRITUAL EXPRESSION

If you became a Christian as an adult, you probably still remember your first awkward attempts to pray out loud before a group. Maybe you're still struggling in that area. In the same way, some don't feel comfortable discussing what God is doing in their lives, or the latest passage of Scripture they read, while standing in line at the supermarket.

Children, as a rule, find such conversations more matter-of-fact but still may find public praying embarrassing. You can help by allowing them to see you pray in the living room with your husband, over the phone with a friend, even at the fast food joint before you bite into the hamburger and french fries. Strive to make conversation with God an everyday, at-any-moment occurrence.

ENCOURAGE THEM TO KEEP SEEING GOD'S POINT OF VIEW

Sometimes it's a long time between spiritual thoughts for a kid. Even a child who gives full attention to Sunday morning lessons might not get his mind back to God again until some crucial problem hits him.

Simple reminders such as "God can help you remember that spelling word, if you ask Him" or "Wow, didn't the Lord give us a beautiful day?" sprinkled in a day can prompt our children to think of Him often.

HELP THEM LOVE TO READ

The love of reading is one of the greatest legacies any mother can leave her children. Listen to them read. Help them grow in confidence with their use of words.

Besides all the other great books for children available these days, introduce them to Bible stories, biographies, short devotional books, and good Christian fiction, such as *Pilgrim's Progress*, by John Bunyan, and *The Chronicles of Narnia*, by C. S. Lewis. Buy each child a Bible he can read for himself, such as *The Living Bible* paraphrase.

PRAY WITH THEM

The best time for Janet to pray with Aaron seems to be at night when he's ready for bed. But, she admits, that's often the time she's most tired and impatient. She's tempted at times to pass over this duty or pray in a hurry. But Aaron insists on proper treatment. He's still at the stage when he wants her to pray with him. He's not quite sure God will hear his prayers in the same way without her.

On Steve and Aaron's "buddy night," they share a brief devotion and prayer time too. Aaron's requests expand from "a good night's sleep and good dreams" when Mom prays, to "please help Mindy to get well and help Tim not to be so lonesome without his Daddy" when Dad prays with him. Perhaps he feels Dad has the most pull in heaven.

When a prayer is answered, write down the circumstance and date in a notebook as a further reinforcement.

Memorized prayers are all right in the beginning, but gently urge children to express their feelings, desires, and struggles in their own words, when they're ready.

Ask your child to pray for you and Dad on special occasions. Let them know you think their prayers are important.

DEALING WITH OBSTACLES

IF YOUR HUSBAND DOESN'T DO HIS PART

When your husband is uninterested in spiritual things, it puts you in a tough situation, but this may be just temporary. With that in mind, try a positive approach.

Whenever possible, pull him into the spiritual conversations. Something along the lines of "Honey, we were talking about why God made an appendix. Do you have any ideas?"

Try to find subjects in which he can be knowledgeable. Don't purposely expose his weaknesses. Help him to get used to being considered the spiritual authority in the home.

Privately talk to him about what role you need him to fulfill. Don't assume that he ought to know what to do. Don't assume that you both mean the same thing when you talk about one of you tackling the spiritual teaching chores, and the other encouraging. Explain what you mean. Listen to him. Get his views on the subject. Find out why he feels the way he does.

Offer your assistance to help him fulfill his role. If he doesn't know where to begin to talk to the children about spiritual things, rummage around at the Christian bookstore for some reading materials he and the kids can work on together. Remind him of family films or seminars at the church. But if he gives you the longsuffering "you're nagging me" look, back off. Give the matter over to God in trusting prayer.

Let him know you appreciate what he is doing with and for the kids. Affirm those positive qualities that make him a good dad. Don't make him feel he's a failure in your eyes because of one neglected area. That is for your sake, as well as his. The more you emphasize the good he does, the less irritating the weakness will be.

IF YOU HAVE A HOSTILE HUSBAND

A nonspiritual, even antagonistic, husband puts you in a very difficult spot.

Continue, with much sensitivity, the children's Christian education. Pray for much wisdom and grace to instruct your children in the truth of Christ without openly stirring your husband's wrath. That will not be healthy for any of you. You can still have a great influence on their future spiritual decisions, even without your husband's backing, but the challenge is great.

Find a sympathetic, trusted friend who can back you up in prayer and perhaps counsel, maybe someone who has had a similar situation. You will need an encourager too.

Do not put down his lack of spiritual awareness in front of the kids. And don't blurt out to the whole church family that your heathen husband needs to be saved. He will not appreciate hearing that by the grapevine. Find a very few, select, spiritually mature friends in which you can confide.

Make sure your children have contact with spiritually mature dads. They might see such a role model at Sunday school or a midweek club meeting or, perhaps, through a camping or other field trip experience.

Make sure you are not neglecting his personal needs. A dad who is content that he is loved, cared for, and appreciated usually doesn't complain too much about church meetings and devotional times at home. But start to ignore the laundry and meals and have a headache every night and no wonder he becomes contentious about where you do spend your time and attention.

Pray for him. Pray that his heart and mind will be open to understand the truth of who Christ is and what He requires of him. Pray for God's grace to him in his daily pressures on the job and for the private things he may not feel free to share with you. Pray for yourself to be free from anger and bitterness at his attitude toward a very vital part of your life, your commitment to Christ.

IF YOU HAVE NO HUSBAND

If you have no husband, you will have to be both teacher and encourager. The role of spiritual teacher may not seem to fit you, but with God's help, do your best. With a job and all the many other duties and hassles, you may not have the desire or strength to add any such undertaking. Then don't allow it to become such a big burden. Pray for opportunities to instruct your children as you're with them a few minutes here, a few minutes there. Take advantage of unexpected moments of quiet or aloneness with each child to listen to what's happening with him and give guidance where you can.

Place your children under the influence of spiritually mature dads whenever possible, and seek out prayer partners. For those who feel an excessive weight on them to carry the whole load of the spiritual welfare of their children, the Scriptures have some refreshing news.

Paul said in Philippians 1:6 of his "spiritual children": "For I am confident of this very thing, that He who began a good work in you will perfect it until the day of Christ Jesus."

The children in our home are really God's children. And it is His work in them that will prod them back on the right track and keep them going. Take confidence in His mighty promises of help and guidance. All He asks is that you dole out your words and actions of encouragement as you have the opportunity.

That's all any good mom can do.

11

Boys Don't Hit Girls

"What's the difference between girls and boys?" challenged a recreational director to several dozen youngsters.

"Girls have longer hair."

"Boys get dirtier."

"Girls giggle."

"Boys push."

"Girls can't throw a baseball very far."

"Boys are lousy at jumping rope."

"Girls like to play with dolls."

"Boys like scary cartoons on TV."

Finally, one boy concluded with what he considered the definitive word. "Listen, here's the main difference. Boys can't hit girls." As far as Teddy Smithwright was concerned, that said it all.

All the children were right about one thing. Girls and boys are different.

Genesis 1:27 states that "God created man in His own image, in the image of God He created him; male and female He created them."

Male and female. No matter what culture, era, or civilization we live in, two distinct facets of humanity coexist. Moms have the privilege of helping their children to understand, appreciate, and honor the distinctions.

Margo arrived at church yesterday sporting a bright pink ribbon in her hair. What a feat. No one would have guessed that she had enough hair to hold a ribbon. At six weeks old, she didn't, but her mom found a way for the bow to stay in place almost all morning. Distinction between the sexes begins early.

Twenty-year-old Michael rushed into the living room to see his mother. "I'm late for work—does this tie look all right with this shirt?" He didn't bother asking Dad. He wanted a woman's opinion. He had no intention of leaving home before he knew that at least one woman approved of his selection.

What should we be teaching our children about their roles? We're told today that there should be no separate roles, that males and females are basically alike. But doesn't that require sweeping generalization based on a few exceptions? And doesn't that add unnecessary stress to our children when we open them up to compete and usurp roles they're not made to perform? Separate domains make for peace and unity. Invasion of domains makes for war.

ROLE GUIDELINES

How can you best instruct your children in order to help nourish a healthy society and produce well balanced individuals? Let's consider.

SOCIAL ROLES

Social roles do vary from culture to culture, but they're crucial for social interaction, unity, and vitality. The Bible has little to say about the specifics of such behavior, but it has much to say about our social attitudes. As we study the Scriptures we can apply them to our own society's expected outer conduct.

Boys

They're never too young (or too old) to learn graces such as:

- holding the door open for ladies
- walking on the curb side of the street
- standing when ladies enter the room

- offering their chair when the room is crowded
- holding her chair when she sits or stands.

We tend to assume that these skills will either be learned automatically or that they are too antiquated for our present generation. Both assumptions are wrong.

Teach your children to respect other children's parents. Especially teach your teenage sons to show respect to the parents of girls they date. Have you ever noticed how suspicious dads and moms become as their daughters turn into young ladies? Boys must learn to respect the rules of another household. They must learn to appreciate the wisdom and opinion of a girl's parents.

It has been said that lack of effective communication is key to almost every problem in life. Don't wait until your children are of dating age to begin such instruction. Teach them while they are young how to initiate conversation with a friend's parents. Help them learn to verbally show appreciation for the kindness shown by a friend's mom or dad.

Teach your sons courteous table manners. From what we see of our present society, such politeness that was taken for granted a generation ago has greatly diminished. Other than wiping the milkshake off the upper lip and saying, "Excuse me," when belching at the table, few fellows seem to know much about simple etiquette. Little things like sitting up straight, elbows off the table, napkin in the lap, waiting for everyone to be served, and which fork to use seem to be lost art forms. Just learning to say, "No, thank you," instead of, "Yuck!" would make a marked difference around many dinner tables (including ours).

Girls

Teach your daughter the difference between making friends with boys and having a boyfriend.

A girl who has some brothers close to her in age has an advantage. A girl who has some good friends who happen to be boys has an even greater advantage. By ten a girl should know how to initiate a conversation with a boy. By thirteen she should know to do more than giggle when a boy's around.

Help your daughter discover ways to find and discuss things of interest with every boy she meets. Help her enjoy the varied background and resources of every relationship without sizing up each one as a potential date to the prom. That doesn't mean she has to become a whiz at fixing carburetors or memorize last year's football statistics. It does mean that she knows how to get a boy talking about such topics if they are important to him, and she knows how to pick up on his excitement for them.

Teach your daughter to be a gracious hostess. Whether she gets married at twenty or forty or never, it is inconceivable that she will never have to be a hostess of one type or another. She will have a house or an apartment or a condo. She might live downtown, in the suburbs, or in the middle of the wilderness, but she will have guests in her home.

You'll find most girls receptive to such teaching at an early age. Lining up three dolls around the table for a tea party is not merely a child's diversion, it's a training exercise for life.

Last December a young mother we know hosted a Christmas tea with her nine-year-old daughter. Mom invited a number of her friends, and so did Joy. They prepared the invitations together, cleaned the house, baked the goodies, set the tables, placed the decorations, and greeted their guests together. The party entertainment included an ornament gift exchange. Joy and her friends had the happy duty of passing out numbers and packages. This young lady is learning by doing.

A daughter should be taught early how and why to dress well. At the same time she should understand that as a person she is of much higher importance than anything she may wear. One of the chief functions of clothing, besides protection, is to aid those around us in focusing their attention on us as valued persons, not objects to ogle.

There's nothing biblical about wearing clothes that are twenty years behind the times. Let her wear the fashion of the day, and teach her to find the best styles and colors for her shape and skin tone. Help her with such practical ideas as picking out new clothes that will match and complement those already in her wardrobe.

Take her to fashion shows or enroll with her in a "dress for success" class. She'll gain confidence as she relaxes in the area of outward appearance.

PHYSICAL ROLES

The great push of our day is to obliterate male and female distinc-tives. We're breaking out of stereotypes, crashing out of molds. That's not all bad. Some good emerges through exciting vocation opportunities, more equitable pay, less harassment.

But some things change to our great detriment. The soul of our so-ciety relies upon our deference to the sexes.

Boys

Teddy Smithwright was correct. Boys don't hit girls. At age six, most girls can stand toe to toe with a boy and slug it out. By age twelve the girls just might have the edge. But by eighteen Junior has them by sixty to one hundred pounds and about six to ten inches. The hitting match is no longer on equal terms. If Teddy's dictum were firmly practiced, we wouldn't be contending with the wide-spread battered wife syndrome.

Somewhere along the line we've lost the vision of true masculin-ity. It's either "macho man" or "wimp" these days. Neither image is very manly, nor is either biblical.

In Mark 10 Jesus is teaching a multitude when He's interrupted by some mothers pushing their little ones toward Him. The disciples sprang up in protest. But Jesus "was indignant and said to them, 'Per-mit the children to come to Me; do not hinder them, for the king-dom of God belongs to such as these' " (v. 14). Then He "took them in His arms" (v. 16)—the gentle Jesus.

But there's more to Jesus than that. In the next chapter (Mark 11) Jesus enters the great Temple at Jerusalem. He looks around Him, enraged at the perversion He sees.

"And He entered the temple and began to cast out those who were buying and selling in the temple, and overturned the tables of the moneychangers and the seats of those who were selling doves" (v. 15).

A companion passage in John 2:15 says that "He made a scourge of cords, and drove them all out of the temple." This Jesus had a whip in hand and a look in His eye that made grown men run for fear.

Gentleness is self-control. It's knowing both the right time and the wrong time to get angry. That's one mark of true manhood.

Some injustices and desecrations are worthy of our anger. That's what Jesus taught us. But we would have to sort through a lot of daily irritations before we would find anything remotely comparable. At the same time our children need to know that we're on their side, that we care about the things that bother them.

Teach your son to defend the women in his life. Some would call this an archaic chivalry. It's not. It's common respect. A civilized society should provide an atmosphere in which women do not have to live in constant fear of physical harm. That doesn't mean that women are always physically weaker than men. And it doesn't imply that women should never learn how to defend themselves. But there may be times to step between the rock throwing bully on the playground and little sister.

We read a recent account of a would-be rapist who was foiled by a five-year-old boy. The attacker broke into a woman's home and grabbed her, but her son leveled a family shotgun at him and convinced him to let his mother go. That may be an extreme example, but the principle stands.

Girls

A healthy female can do most anything she sets her mind to. But it's just a waste of time for her to try to compete against every male. God didn't make a mistake. A female is created to complement a male, not overpower him. We can appreciate the similarities and be proud of the differences.

Women need to accept the limits of their physical brawn and the peripheries of their physical looks. Let your daughter in on a secret few women understand. To men, the most attractive women are the ones who are not possessed by thoughts about themselves. It's the woman who enjoys herself, accepts her own looks, and cares enough not to abuse what God has given her that is always most appealing to men.

Teach her not to use her body as a tool or a weapon. At some age she has to learn, from Mom, that boys are sexually stimulated by the sight of the female body. She should not use her body to get attention, to get her way, or to obtain favors.

The young lady who uses physical flirtation to get her way as she grows up will probably use her body as a weapon against her husband later in life. There's no quicker way to mess up a marriage.

MENTAL/EMOTIONAL ROLES

Boys

Help your son know what to say and what not to say to a girl. Let him know that words are powerful; words can destroy; words can cripple; words can ruin days, weeks, months, and even years.

Teach him to watch harsh speech. It's not just a matter of language. Anything that should not be discussed in the presence of women should not be discussed in public at all. Harsh speech is more than foul language or thundering volume. It has to do with tone and attitude. There are few women who couldn't hear the inflection through the words. A woman may easily forget what he said but never forget how he said it.

From the time they play blocks with the girl next door, let your son know that it is never right to make fun of the way a girl looks.

Sherri is thirty-two years old, has three little girls, a loving husband, and a house with an adjoining corral for her horses. Sherri also has anorexia. She has a dread of getting fat. She says that if she eats too much all the fat goes to her thighs. Why can't she relax about it?

Part of it stems back to Dwight Hayword. He sat in front of her during freshman high school English. She overheard him laughing with the other boys once. He told them, "Oh, Sherri. Sure, she has a cute smile, but she has fat thighs." No one, in almost twenty years, has been able to convince her otherwise.

Teach your son to listen to a girl's opinions. At some point in life he's got to discover that girls are not stupid. Most of them can be very wise, bright, and witty.

Boys are not, and should not attempt to sound like, experts on every important subject on earth. Every girl has her expertise. She may also have an intuition that baffles the male mind.

Just two miles from the beach, Benny's car stopped running. He coasted over to the side of the road and got out to search for a solution. But everything was dead. There was no electrical power at all. His girl friend, Lori, finally suggested, "I think your trouble is in the glove compartment."

It was so ridiculous, Benny didn't even bother responding. He checked the battery; it was charged. He cleaned the cables. He inspected the alternator, the distributor, and the coil. He was flat on his back under the car, mutilating his new surfing shirt on the asphalt when Lori spoke up again. "I really think it's in the glove compartment."

Benny crawled out and flared out in disgust at Lori's obvious ignorance of auto mechanics. The tirade over, he finished with, "What on earth makes you even say such a thing?"

"Well, I was looking at the map to see how much farther to the ocean, and when I put the map back in and closed the glove compartment, that's when the car died. And, see, right there at the back? There are a couple little wires back there. Do you suppose they are supposed to be joined together?"

Benny pushed the separated coupling back together, instantly started the car, and mumbled all the way to the beach.

Some guys seem to be born with sensitivity, the ability to really understand how another person feels. Most men, however, have to learn the skill. Too many want to take everything literally. They don't take time to get below the surface.

He says, "How do you feel?"

She says, "Uh, fine. I guess."

"Great," he replies, "let's spend the day at the car races." But she isn't fine. She's depressed. She wants to talk about it, but she's not sure he wants to listen. She's hoping he'll sense it so they can spend some quiet time alone. The race track will definitely not do.

"Hey," he states, "she said she was fine. How was I supposed to know?"

Sensitivity, for many, is a learned skill. No one can teach it better than professionals at being sensitive. No one can teach it better than Mom.

Girls

A girl's emotions are God given. There's nothing wrong with crying during sad films, being more worried about the little baby in the third row than who's in the batter's box, or insisting that everyone buckle the seat belt on the short trip to the supermarket. Empathy, compassion, and healthy respect for potential danger are acceptable responses.

In the process, teach a daughter the difference between emotions and emotionalism. The whining, crying, complaining woman who teeters on the verge of emotional collapse can wear down others quickly.

Our emotions are never wrong. They are a true statement about how we feel at any moment. But what we do with our emotions can be either right or wrong. Anytime our emotional response to a scene, thought, or action leads us to react according to biblical principles or to building the character of Christ within, then the emotion has been a positive, necessary force in our lives.

Teach your daughter endurance. She needs to learn to get tough —not insensitive, not callous, not harsh—just tough. Your little darling in the pink ruffles cannot be protected by some sterile existence. Up ahead there are going to be disappointments, trials, suffering, pain, and grief. That's the kind of world we have created for ourselves. It's not going to change until the day the Lord returns.

Prepare her to turn to the Lord God for her strength and wisdom. Teach her to see the whole spectrum of a life, instead of just the catastrophe of the day. Help her to understand that virtue and happiness are never measured by who starts out the fastest but rather by who crosses the finish line still holding onto both.

Teach her flexibility. That perfect plan for her life, which she has been designing since she was five, just might have to be altered. That ideal husband, formed from an old romantic novel read when she was twelve, just might not be realistic. The big house on the hill might always be beyond grasp. That's all right. Plans can change, sometimes for the better.

However, let her know that flexibility is different from compromise. Compromise means giving in to something you know to be wrong. She must realize that no love in the world should ever make her back away from the commands of God.

SPIRITUAL ROLES

Just as there are social, physical and emotional roles, so there are spiritual roles as well. Clarity of teaching and training in this area is vital.

Boys

Groom boys to be spiritual leaders. First Timothy 3:1-13 tells about the qualities needed to be a leader in the church fellowship. Ephesians 5:22-33 shows that the same qualities are needed to be a spiritual leader in the home.

Are these qualities that can be taught? Certainly. A son must come to his own personal decision to accept Jesus Christ as Lord and Savior. Then he is ready to understand what his role is now and will be in the future within the church fellowship.

Can a mom really guide a young man to understand such things? Not only a mom, but a grandmother as well.

"For I am mindful of the sincere faith within you, which first dwelt in your grandmother Lois, and your mother Eunice, and I am sure that it is in you as well" (2 Timothy 1:5).

Teach them how much they are to love their future wives. "Husbands, love your wives just as Christ also loved the church and gave Himself up for her" (Ephesians 5:25).

It is absurd to think that we can raise our children until they are of marriageable age, give them a microwave oven, and push them out the door to manage on their own. Loving a wife as tenderly and sacrificially as the Lord loves the fellowship is not learned during a honeymoon.

Teach them while they are young. Help them understand that true love means giving without expecting anything in return. Give them some practice in learning how to love like that. Keep drilling into them that married love will require them to give up time, habits, and possessions in the interest of making marriage work.

Girls

"Wives be subject to your own husbands, as to the Lord" (Ephesians 5:22).

This is not a cultural phenomenon limited to the first century. It's not an outdated social structure that is repressive to modern women. It's a mandate for Christians, and when put into practice in the right spirit, it works wonders.

If it's in God's Word, then it is not only correct, it is the best possible way to live. The problem is not, How can we get around obeying this command? But rather, How can we understand and obey it so thoroughly that we achieve all the fullness of joy and abundance that God intended?

This does not teach the inferiority of women. It is a command about the relationship of one man and one woman in marriage. One great fear every mom has concerns her children's happiness in marriage. If a young lady fails to understand the principle of permitting her husband to be leader in the home, she will have a great handicap in achieving the full potential of her marriage.

Teach her that she is a highly gifted young lady and that the Lord expects some of those gifts to be used in the fellowship of believers. "But to each one is given the manifestation of the Spirit for the common good" (1 Corinthians 12:7).

God has called men to be the main spiritual leaders in church and home, but they will not succeed without the many tremendous spiritual gifts, talents, and ministries of the women complementing their own.

What do boys do? What do girls do?

They have certain roles to fulfill within God's wide boundaries.

Good moms will guide each individual child with loving discernment and watchful care.

12

But Mom, There's Nothing to Do!

Three heavy shop tables crowd out the major part of the dining room. They're covered with what could be one of the largest private layouts of Lego building blocks in the Western Hemisphere.

A modest sized adjoining bedroom contains a desk, a large bookcase, two toy chests, and a wall length closet, all crammed full of toys, games, and books. The living room TV corner holds a display of twenty-three video games and a dozen cartoon video tapes. The garage houses a nice assortment of basketballs, baseballs, footballs, soccer balls, and accompanying paraphernalia.

Out back there's a playhouse, a swing set, and a convoy of Tonka trucks. Within three houses on either side of the cul-de-sac live a dozen other children.

Yet in the kitchen of this home a seven-year-old boy mopes, almost in tears, as he insists to his mother, "I'm bored; there's nothing to do!"

Nothing to do? Mom can't even remember a time when she had nothing to do. She'd give her food processor, ironing board, and twenty-five pounds of laundry detergent just to have a couple of days with nothing to do.

This scene in the Bly home is not unique. Almost every home in the country repeats it. Are moms really supposed to be activity directors too? Don't they have enough to do without having to entertain and fill their child's every free moment?

Well, every mom is a teacher. The current push for what is officially called "home schooling" is, in a way, misleading. It assumes you either give your child an education at home, or you push him out into the world to be taught. The truth is, whether your child goes to public school, private school, or learns his ABC's at home, the most important part of his education takes place under his own roof.

Children can be taught how to play. They can be taught how to spend their time. They can be taught how to find enjoyable activities on their own.

Many folks complain about the fact that modern conveniences such as television rob kids of initiative and creativity. They develop a passive "entertain me" mindset, they say. They may be right. But complaining isn't enough. We've got to develop countermeasures that effectively balance this tendency.

We don't have to entertain our children. We don't have to be constantly racking our brains for some new activity for them. How much better to spend some time to teach them how to discover fun and helpful activities on their own.

Most kids are quick learners. All we have to do is encourage, challenge, and channel all that potential creative energy.

Creativity can be learned. Having imaginative, highly creative children is not merely a matter of genetic composition. An inventor like Thomas Edison is universally hailed as a creative genius. However, it was not on his first try that he invented the incandescent light bulb. A few thousand attempts preceded the one that worked.

Why take time to build creativity? Because, of all the lessons in education they are going to learn, none will better prepare them to be a future productive success than developing creativity. Nothing will better prepare them to experience the abundance God has in store for them. Nothing will better help them to be an enjoyable companion. Nothing will make them more useful for service within the family, church, and community. And besides that, nothing will better help them think up something fun on those boring days with "nothing to do."

THINGS TO DO

So how do you go about it? One or more of these suggestions might be a place to start.

TRAVEL

Take them places. You wouldn't think of letting your child miss out on four years of school. But some folks don't bat an eye at missing four years' worth of vacations. You might take short trips to the parks, museums, and zoos or long trips to the mountains, lakes, and oceans. You can take trips to the farm and trips to the big city. You can go to the airport and watch the big planes take off or go to the marshes and watch the ducks land.

Obviously next Tuesday, right before dinner, when you're in the middle of baking a week's casseroles and scraping off old wallpaper, is not the time you are going to stop and take the kids to the beach. But a life-style that includes regular travel means more overall creativity at home.

Aaron spent two weeks digging a huge ditch across his backyard play yard. "Look, Mom, it's the Grand Canyon," he announced. It had been a year since we gaped at the rim of that majestic creation, but the thoughts were still inspiring him.

PROBLEM SOLVING

No kid should have life delivered to him or her on a silver plate —or even on a paper plate, for that matter. You don't have to unravel every mystery, open every package, or assemble every toy for them.

From the earliest years on, find activities that encourage exploration. How do things work? Why does it rattle? How can you make it roll better? Is there any way to build a taller building? How do you open this box? What makes the clock work?

As they grow older, give them bigger problems. How should we decorate your room? How can we organize the toys better? How are you going to decide which one of your stuffed animals goes on vacation with us?

The question about which stuffed animal should go on vacation was creatively solved recently by a little friend of ours. She decided that all the animals in her room should vote to elect a representative to accompany the family on vacation. Two candidates were selected: Stewart, her favorite stuffed cat, and Fresno, a rather naughty bear. There was campaigning. Speeches were made, ballots cast, and votes counted. The final tally was seventeen to two in favor of Stewart.

Melodie explained, "Stewart, being a nice cat, voted for Fresno."

It was no surprise to the family that Stewart was the winner. They all knew Melodie would pick him. But the process took up the better part of an afternoon, and Melodie's mother was thoroughly delighted with her creativity.

ACTIVE READING

Don't get upset if your children continually struggle to memorize dates, events, and scientific terms. But do everything within your ability to help them learn to read. Reading opens up the world that God has created. Reading opens up the Word of God, which, in itself, is sufficient for "everything we need for life and godliness" (2 Peter 1:3).

Active reading means books, books, and more books. It means not waiting for them to be old enough to read, but reading to them yourself. It means regular trips to the library, where they should feel at home. Teach them that it is as exciting and thrilling to walk down the aisle of a well-stocked library as it is to walk down the aisle of a toy store.

Active reading means buying them books. Take them to the Christian bookstore and let them discover the many creative choices available. They should have as many Christian books as you do. Books are expensive. You might want to utilize or even organize a library in your church. But even if you have to spend extra to purchase books, it will be worthwhile. When they are grown and away at college, you may be paying several hundred dollars a year just for their books. Those books might not contain any positive reference to God at all. Wouldn't it be a shame if during their growing up years you spent more money on non-Christian, even anti-Christian books, than you did on ones that help them discover real life in Christ?

Active reading means reacting to what they read. Discuss the content, conclusions, and pictures. Show empathy with the characters. Look up the places described on a large map.

Challenge the conclusions to see if they are true to God's Word. After reading about a boy and his kite, buy your own and try to fly it.

ACTIVE WRITING

Active writing is the companion to active reading. Encourage your children to express their thoughts and ideas on paper.

Many people don't know how to write. They may know some of the rules of grammar. They may have learned to spell. They might have been able to compose enough sentences, paragraphs, and pages to pass a class called English. But they don't know how to communicate clearly from their minds to the mind of another. That's what writing is all about.

One way to help teach your children to do that is by encouraging them to write their own thank-you notes and letters. Help them think of what to say if they're having a hard time, but let them say it their way. Give them stamped, addressed envelopes to all the grandmas and grandpas or whoever. Let them write a note to cousin Benjy on his birthday. Let them experience the fun and excitement of personal communication.

Another idea is to buy them a nicely bound blank journal book and encourage them to consistently write down their thoughts and experiences of the day. Read their entries and compliment them on their efforts.

High schools often have curriculum entitled "college prep." The idea is that such classes will get you ready for future education. Yet the most important college prep skills, such as active reading and writing, are usually tacked on as extra credit or as year-end projects to be rushed through in the final weeks. Good moms get a jump on this laxity and open the books and notepaper at home.

HOBBIES

It's not really a conspiracy, but more the natural fallout of an electronic, fast-paced society. Nonetheless, good old-fashioned hobbies have faded almost out of existence—hobbies like stamp collecting, gathering rocks, mounting butterflies, making dolls, and digging for seashells.

Maybe the hobbies are still there but are just more sophisticated. Now kids collect Transformers and Barbie Dolls and become experts in video games.

Here are a few guidelines for good hobbies.

- Find an activity that doesn't require constant purchases.
- Look for a hobby that increases personal skills. (For eye-hand coordination try woodworking or making pottery.)
- Give first priority to hobbies that could last into adulthood (photography, rock hounding).
- Discover local groups or classes that would help a child learn more about his hobby.
- Allow your child to become the expert in this field. Encourage him to share his knowledge with the rest of the family. ("Junior is the expert on collecting snakes in our family.")

FIND CREATIVE PEOPLE

Expose your kids to people who are creative. Creativity breeds creativity. If the old man down the street builds exquisite dollhouses in his garage, take Sissy down to watch him work. If Mrs. Davenport knows the sound and look of every bird in ten Western states, see if she would give the kids a tour of the local lakeshore. Invite the new family on the block over for dinner and have the kids listen as Mr. Robertson explains how he designs engines for space rockets.

Your child might not end up wanting to get involved in any of these particular fields, but it will open his eyes to all the possibilities.

Along this line, don't hesitate to stop and take the guided tours at power plants, factories, lumber mills, and similar places. There's a big world out there and a big God to help them discover what they can be.

Now, any busy mom (is there any other kind?) can see that a lot of these suggestions involve doing things with your kids. But, you say, this chapter began with hints about finding ways to keep your children busy so you can do your own thing. Don't worry, we'll get to that. Indirectly. You see, kids that have plenty of creative experiences with Mom, Dad, and the family will have a much easier time with innovations of their own during those slack times when no one else is available.

Yelling at the kids, "Go to your room until dinner. Do something, anything, just leave me alone," only frustrates both of you.

Janet finds spontaneous creativity a real chore. A writing assignment that takes Steve two hours may require two weeks for her. She proudly wears a button that blares "I Don't Do Crafts" for the benefit of all her seamstress, glue-gun, and stencil friends. Since she sometimes finds herself short of originality when fighting the "I have nothing to do" syndrome, she relies heavily on the "let's go see" solution.

Aaron whines, "I have nobody to play with." Janet takes him by the hand, and they begin with his closet. One by one she points out each game and each box of toys. Many times he'll be reminded right away of something he hasn't played with for a long time, and he's off and running. If that doesn't work, they file through the bookcase, one book at a time, to look for something he can read or scan himself.

Then, once in a great while, they have to resort to the "big brother game cupboard." That's where we store the puzzles and games that Russell and Mike left behind. Some intriguing treasure in there entertains for an hour or two until a neighbor boy knocks at the door or a favorite TV show comes on or Mom finally has time for a game of Uno.

This process takes some effort on her part but accomplishes what they both want: Aaron's busy with something fun, and Janet can return to working on a chapter in *How to Be a Good Mom*.

Children—and adults—who take the time to develop a life-style of creativity are rarely bored. As they grow older, out of the whirl of activities and enterprises in which they have engaged themselves, they'll begin to look forward with great anticipation to those rare moments when they have "nothing to do." Also, Mother's role will greatly diminish, as they strike off more and more on their own initiative. Then comes another problem—helping them choose between an ever widening array of alternatives.

MAKING DECISIONS

Children should practice making decisions of their own. When they're ready, they should pick out their own clothes for the day, decide which programs they'll watch for their hour's allotment of TV, or make a commitment between a visit to Grandma's or a trip to Disneyland. They're getting practice in the difficult process that lies ahead of such things as choosing to turn right or left on the roadway, whether to move here or there, and deciding which car to purchase. How do we help them decide?

How about introducing them, one point at a time, to the following test.

SIX POINT BIBLE TEST

1. *Does it pass the wisdom test?* Wisdom is not only knowing the best end goal but also knowing the best method for getting there. Wisdom concerns itself as much with how you get there, as with where you are going.

If we ask God for wisdom, He will grant it.

"But if any of you lacks wisdom, let him ask of God, who gives to all men generously and without reproach, and it will be given to him" (James 1:5).

James also tells us what God's wisdom looks like:

"But the wisdom from above is first pure, then peaceable, gentle, reasonable, full of mercy and good fruits, unwavering, without hypocrisy" (3:17).

When the question arises, "Is this what God really wants me to do?" the right answer will always fit these standards.

2. *Does it pass the purity test?* What thoughts does this activity produce in the mind? Have them answer, "When I think about doing this I feel like—" or, "When I have done this before, it made me—"

Paul said, "Finally, brethren, whatever is true, whatever is honorable, whatever is right, whatever is pure, whatever is lovely, whatever is of good repute, if there is any excellence and if anything worthy of praise, let your mind dwell on these things" (Philippians 4:8).

Principles like this one, taught at an early age, motivate and shape a strong Christian conscience.

3. Does it pass the joy test? The Christian life is not a morbid cling-ing to the hope of a vague, distant future while being overcome by the misery of today. It is not a condemnation to a lifetime of self-degradation.

To be holy does not mean dejection and such stringent toeing the line that there's no place for fun.

Jesus told us clearly, "I came that they might have life, and might have it abundantly" (John 10:10).

That means a life full of purpose, meaning, and vitality. But we've got to choose His way to find His abundance.

Jesus also said, "These things I have spoken to you, that My joy may be in you, and that your joy may be made full" (John 15:11).

Joy is more than a few giggles, a moment's blush of pleasure, and ten years of remorse. Joy is a deeply satisfying contentment that comes with an open heart, mind, and soul relationship with the creator God. Any activity that clouds or strips us of that kind of joy should be trashed.

4. Does it pass the maturity test? Does this action in some way lead to spiritual progress? Or does it mean a backward or static position in growing in knowledge and experience of Christ?

The Bible says our goal should be: "Until we all attain to the unity of the faith, and of the knowledge of the Son of God, to a mature man, to the measure of the stature which belongs to the fullness of Christ" (Ephesians 4:13).

Have them ask the question, "Will this action increase or decrease my spiritual life?"

5. Does it pass the heavenward test? As long as we live and breathe on this planet, we must live in the world. But, the Scriptures inform us, we are not to be "of the world."

"Do not love the world, nor the things in the world. If anyone loves the world, the love of the Father is not in him. For all that is in the world, the lust of the flesh and the lust of the eyes and the boast-ful pride of life, is not from the Father, but is from the world" (1 John 2:15-16).

That means we don't buy into the world's system but keep working to cooperate with God's interests, God's plans, and God's purpose for our personal lives.

"And do not be conformed to this world, but be transformed by the renewing of your mind, that you may prove what the will of God is, that which is good and acceptable and perfect" (Romans 12:2).

This is probably the hardest test. Everything we touch and taste and hear is in some way connected to the material, sensual terrain we must move in. And just because it is material or sensual does not necessarily make it wrong. In addition, the list of dos and don'ts by various sincere Christians further confuses the matter for a concerned mom.

Each one must (a) search the Scriptures, (b) seek the guidance of trusted Christian brothers and sisters, and, (c) pray earnestly for God's direction. Anyone who takes the time and effort to follow these three steps will have no trouble aligning heart and mind heavenward.

6. *Does it pass the kingdom test?* God's army does not march in place, learning mock drills to demonstrate on some heavenly parade ground. There's work to do here on earth. We've been given a task to complete.

Jesus didn't mince words when He said, "Go therefore and make disciples of all the nations, baptizing them in the name of the Father and the Son and the Holy Spirit, teaching them to observe all that I commanded you; and lo, I am with you always, even to the end of the age" (Matthew 28:19-20).

Every crisis decision in life, every major action, every crucial selection must be tested with this command. Will this help expand Christ's kingdom? Where does this fit into His kingdom plans?

Are moms activity directors?

They should be much more than that. When Junior cries out, "Mom, I'm bored, there's nothing to do!" he's really saying, "Mom, I need you to make all my decisions for me."

You know it's time to take him by the hand and look with him at all the options. Then, he must settle himself in place as he makes himself at home in the world of choices.

Well done, Mom.

13

Yes, I'm Going Out with Daddy, *Alone*

The night of Janet's birthday Steve surprised her with an overnight stay at a beautiful southern California resort overlooking the crashing waves of the Pacific Ocean.

"Well, what did you do?" Aaron asked when they returned.

"We had a picnic dinner, viewed the sunset on the ocean from our balcony patio, and watched an old movie on television. Then we slept in late the next morning, had a nice breakfast, and came home," Jan reported.

"That's all?" Aaron sounded disbelieving. "Didn't you swim in the ocean? Didn't you go to the miniature golf course? Didn't you play anything?"

"Well—" Janet hesitated. "We did have a fun time."

"Yeah, it sounds really boring to me." He shrugged.

Part of his disappointment was not at our lack of activity but rather that we had not included him. At his age it's difficult for him to understand that the world does not center on him all the time.

Good moms place a high priority on privacy with dads.

If children resent that time together, it's probably because no one ever sat down to explain the family rules about married life.

THE RULES OF MARRIED LIFE

One rule might be: financial problems are never, never discussed while Mom is in the first days of her monthly period. In fact, Dad should try to remove every element of added stress. Now that rule is not written down anywhere, but it is carefully guarded by the wise husband. The problem is, the kids probably don't know about this rule and so they may get caught in the crunch of wondering, "What's wrong with Mom?"

For the health and happiness of the family unit, the unwritten rules ought to be explained sometime.

Here are some sample rules. You will want to add your own.

1. If any conflicts develop in relationships in the family, the Mom-Dad relationship takes first priority.

Nick drags home, discouraged. His job is going nowhere. It's been ten long years of one draining day after another. He can't see any hope for change in the future. He obviously needs to talk.

His wife, Roxanne, puts down the dress she's hemming and eases into the den to visit with him. It's a long conversation. Years of frustration pour out.

Shellie, their daughter, bursts into the room yelling, "Mom, have you got my dress finished yet? Tony's going to be here any minute now, and I *have* to have that dress!"

"Oh, I'm sorry, honey, your Dad and I need to talk. I won't be able to get it done." Then Roxanne ushers her back out the door.

"But, Mom, what will I wear?" Shellie wails.

"How about the blue chambray, or else you can finish that hem yourself. But I want you to understand very clearly that the conversation your Dad and I are having at the moment is extremely important."

Shellie was sixteen years old, but she needed to understand rule 1.

2. In dealing with the children, Mom and Dad are always on the same side.

Little Nathan was negotiating for the best deal. By last count there were fourteen presents for him under the family Christmas tree. Since that was considerably more than were there for the others, he figured out a way to keep everyone from being jealous of him on Christmas day.

"Why don't I unwrap a present or two before Christmas," he suggested to his mother. "Then it wouldn't look so, you know, unbalanced?"

It sounded quite reasonable to Nathan.

Mom relented, "Oh, I suppose one present wouldn't hurt. But wait and ask your dad."

Nathan was halfway there. When dad tromped through the front door he was barraged with, "Daddy, Mommy thinks it would be a good idea for me to open one of my presents ahead of time, you know, since I have too many anyway. She said it was OK, but that I should ask you. You don't mind, do you?"

Nathan's Dad did mind. "One of the great delights in having presents is the anticipation of opening them. Once you open one, you'll want to open another. Soon, all the good lessons, and most of the fun, are lost. I think we ought to wait until Christmas."

"But Mom said I could!" Nathan appealed.

But Mom's right behind him. "Well, Nate, I think Dad is right. You'd better wait."

"That's no fair! You always take Daddy's side," Nathan whines.

His mother just smiles and nods. "You're right, I'm always on his side."

Nathan had just been struck down, once again, by rule 2.

3. No child was ever damaged by seeing evidence that Mom and Dad love each other.

Tommy's turbo moon rocket blaster was just about to make a successful landing on the alien planet Phlinxtorpe when he heard a strange noise. Was it the evil Spymaster returning to destroy earth? Was it another visit by the sinister Doomlaunch? Perhaps it was Princess Sweetlight trying to make it to safety.

"Nah, it's coming from the living room. Must be the TV," Tommy surmised.

Then, suddenly, the awful thought hit him. He knew what the noise was. "They're in there kissing!" He ran as fast as his legs would scurry in hopes of catching them in the act of the crime. But he was too late. Mom and Dad were sitting next to each other, hugging.

"You've been kissing in here, haven't you?" he accused.

"Oh, well, I suppose we were," his mom said. "Do you call this kissing?" She grabbed her husband and planted a kiss on his lips.

"Hey, that's enough," Tommy protested, "I could hear you clear in my room. Aren't you guys too old for that?"

"Nah." Mom smiled and kissed Dad again.

"Oh, brother." Tommy sighed. "I'm going back to Phlinxtorpe."

"Where?" his father asked.

"The planet Phlinxtorpe. Moms and dads don't kiss on Phlinxtorpe."

"It must be a very lonely place," Mom replied. Poor old Tommy. Chased away by rule 3.

4. Sexual relations between Mom and Dad are private—as well as legal, moral, biblical, and enjoyable.

"Mom, I've got to ask you something." Jennifer tossed down her school books as she slid into the kitchen. "Listen, we had this film at school today, and, well—do you and Dad have sex?"

Jennifer's mom almost dropped her cup of coffee.

"Oh, well, I mean—it's just that this film was, you know, a sex education film. Well, it made sex seem kind of clinical, you know, like going to the doctor, or something. Is that the way it is?"

It was a moment that Jennifer's mom knew would be arriving. She had hoped it wouldn't be quite this soon, or quite this way, but she was determined not to avoid the subject.

"Well, no, actually it's quite romantic. Did you want to talk about it?" She waited for Jennifer to return to the table carrying an apple.

"Yeah." She plopped down to slice and core the apple.

Her mom took a deep breath. "Jennifer, do you know what actually happens when two people love each other in that way?"

"You mean, getting pregnant and all that?"

"Yes, but also, do you know what happens to the man and to the woman while they are making love?"

"Oh, sure. I guess they told us at school. But, not really. What happens?"

Jennifer's mom described the specific details as completely as she thought necessary. Then she asked, "Do you know what the Bible has to say about sex?"

"I suppose. It's kind of naughty, huh?" she questioned.

"No. The Bible says that sex is a wonderful experience given to a husband and a wife in order to produce children and to provide a deep intimacy in their love for each other. As long as people follow God's rules, it's a wonderful thing."

"Rules like, don't mess around until you get married?" said a very direct preteen.

"That's one of the most important rules. But it wasn't given to take away your fun. God knows that when we violate that rule we bring all sorts of trouble upon ourselves and others. He is saying that sex is a special gift that He has reserved for those who are married. Within that relationship it is enjoyable and deeply satisfying. Those who try sex out of the marriage commitment declare that they know more than God about human relationships. It's like a baby playing with fire. Somebody's going to get hurt."

"Mom, is sex scary?"

"Not when it's with your marriage partner. It's a relationship that grows with time. It's really—well, wait until you're married, then you'll know."

"Then you and Dad do have sex—still?"

Jennifer's mom raised her eyebrows. "Yes, we do!"

"I thought so." Jennifer reached into the cupboard for a cookie. Rule 4 was beginning to sink in.

5. Mom and Dad need to get away by themselves on a regular basis.

Barbara happened onto the perfect part-time job. She works while the kids are in school, and, as she puts it, "I make just enough to have a house cleaner come in twice a month, pay the babysitter every week, and have enough leftover for a neat date with my husband. What more could I want?"

She's one smart lady. Every Friday night, without fail, she and her husband have that date.

"But, it's not fair," Kaylee sniffles. "You have Daddy all to yourself."

"Yeah, and it sure is fun," Barbara assures her.

"Well, don't you miss me?" Kaylee prompts.

"We sure do. That's why we need to get away. Just so we can remember how much we miss you! Do you understand?"

"I—I think so." Kaylee sighs.

It's tough to come to grips with rule 5.

6. *Both Mom and Dad will try to give each child consistent private attention.*

Aaron complained loudly about his parents having their night out. It seemed they were having all the fun. Then Dad instigated Buddy Night. Now every Wednesday Aaron and his Dad spend an evening together. It's a trip to the fast food joint, a visit to the park, a game of basketball, a couple books to read, a project to build out in the shop, or a home video to rent. It's just Aaron and Dad, so Fridays don't seem all that lonesome anymore.

Wednesdays work well for Aaron and his Dad because that's the night that Mom directs two handbell choir rehearsals at church and Dad has the fewest meetings.

Rule 6 is working out very well.

7. *Whenever Mom and Dad are out alone, the kids are well taken care of.*

Good babysitters can be difficult to find. That's why the Andersons have latched onto Vickie. She and the three Anderson kids have a great time together.

Mrs. Anderson always makes sure that there's something tasty in the cupboard for dinner, that Vickie knows where to reach them, and that a neighbor is home, just in case of an emergency.

One week she had all the ingredients for chocolate chip cookies laid out and waiting for the gang to make on their own. Another time, newsprint paper and paint awaited the young artists out on the patio.

Mrs. Anderson decided she had a firm handle on rule 7 when her husband's flu forced them to cancel Friday night plans and all the kids cried, "Does this mean that Vickie's not coming over?"

Rules for Single Parents

Single parents, of course, will have to adapt their family rules to their own situation. But, some principles still apply.

1. *Live a biblical life-style.* Make sure your present actions meet with God's standards. No matter what the circumstances of the past, your kids need to see you now striving to do what's right in God's sight.

2. *Demonstrate by failure what success looks like.* If your singleness is a result of separation or divorce, let your kids know what you learned from your mistakes. It is shocking to hear the statistics on the number of children from broken homes who wind up in the same situation themselves. It is as if no lessons were imparted to the next generation.

3. *Keep exhibiting good models for them to see.* In-laws, neighbors, friends, and the folks in the pew ahead of you at church can all be examples. It may sometimes seem awkward for single parents to hang around happily married couples, but do it anyway. Your kids really need to see what makes it work.

4. *Encourage your children to ask questions.* They want to know about marriage, family life, and sex. They might want to know, "What went wrong?" Let them know that such subjects are not off limits. Sure, they may be painful for you to talk about, but the kids have a right to know. Remember, they are the ones paying a price for something over which they had absolutely no control. They deserve the freedom to ask questions.

What's the goal of having time alone with your husband? Perhaps Jesus explained it best.

Jesus did mighty miracles. He taught us about His purpose in coming to earth. He revealed the mysteries of God's kingdom. He also schooled us in the basics of family life. In discussing the closeness of the relationship between husband and wife He quoted from Genesis.

"For this cause a man shall leave his father and mother, and shall cleave to his wife; and the two shall become one flesh" (Matthew 19:5).

"Cleave" may sound rather old-fashioned. It means to adhere to, cling to, stick fast, to be faithful.

Without special equipment a sheer rock cliff is unclimbable. You have to have handholds and footholds of some sort. You need something to cleave onto. Building a strong, healthy, vital marriage is no less difficult than climbing a sheer rock cliff without the proper equipment.

Any man who thinks he can maintain a good marriage by anything else than clutching tightly, in faithfulness, and not letting go, is due for a painful fall.

But dads have to have something to hold onto. At times, it's going to take more than a marriage certificate and a twenty-year-old pledge. He's going to need someone who will listen and encourage, plan and dream, love and embrace. Good moms make time to be with Dad—alone.

14

There's Always a Time to Pull Rank

Becoming a mother is irrevocable.

You can't throw it off. You can't hide it. You can't disguise it. You are forever, in the child's eyes, in the mind of society, and in the annals of heaven, somebody's mom.

No doubt there have been a few (brief, we hope) instances when you've considered ways to disenfranchise yourself from motherhood. Maybe it was during another long pouting session from your teenager or smart aleck retorts from the younger one. Or maybe you still stagger from the baby's long crying spells. We've all had thoughts of resigning.

On the other hand, take a peek at your children's point of view. They've had their own thoughts of replacing mother with a more tolerant substitute. But in either case, replacement is impossible. You are, and will forever be, Mom.

There are some advantages to that state of affairs. Let's take a review of the benefits.

At least for the first twenty years of life, only God knows this child better than you do. You are in an incredible position to experience life with him.

You have the privilege to act "just like a mother." You don't need to explain why you "mother" them when you're twenty or forty or sixty or eighty. You are Mom, and you can be overprotective, over-indulgent, and oversupportive, if you like.

The slightest hint of reassurance from you can inspire them to reach for heady heights.

"Mom thinks I can do it" remains an irrefutable argument. You may be the single greatest human influence their lives will ever have.

But what if you're overwhelmed?

What if everything you've read so far doesn't seem to apply to you?

Maybe your situation's too far gone, or you're new at being a mother, or you feel your own inadequacies too keenly. Wherever you are, there's a way to tell if you've got the potential for being one of the "good" ones.

How to Tell if You Can Be a Good Mom

1. You have your spiritual life in focus. You've established a relation-ship with God through personal trust in Jesus Christ. Your spiritual commitment directly affects and influences everything you do. You know you don't have everything mastered yet, but you're willing to work on it.

2. You're not satisfied with just surviving. You don't want to merely tolerate a situation; you want to enjoy it and benefit from it. You're not content with accepting whatever comes your way, but you're in-tent to discover the meaning and purpose behind it.

3. You believe in ultimate accountability for your days here on earth. You consider the humans within your sphere a part of a divine pur-pose. You feel the glory of your uniqueness, that you could nurture little lives in a way no other person on earth could duplicate.

4. You believe that your own personal happiness depends to a major part on your relationship with your family, even though you find personal pleasure from other sources too. You're committed to the fact that this is the very place God wants you to be in.

5. You trust that when Jesus said (in John 10:10) that He came to give us an abundant life (a life full of joy, purpose, meaning, and satisfaction), He meant to include your family.

It takes a lot of work to be a good mom. The physical load strains your body to its limits. The mental anguish and stress is almost impossible to describe at times. The spiritual battles would overwhelm you if it weren't for the Lord's special grace and strength. But the bottom line still reads the same—it's all worth it.

Some folks don't understand the value of strong family relationships. They keep using the wrong measurements. They say, "Well, you work your whole life, wear yourself out, break your health, and never achieve any recognition—or even enough luxuries to spoil yourself a little. The whole thing's a waste."

Such folks are living a sad lie.

Last February we had a dinner on Janet's birthday. It was a small affair with just Russ and his wife, Lois, Mike and his fiancée, Michelle, and Aaron. Lois prepared the delicious meal of quiche, fresh fruit salad, raw vegetables and dip, huge croissants, and coconut cream and lemon meringue pie for dessert—all of Janet's favorites.

After lunch we hiked a trail along the green foothills and oak trees of southern California. Aaron led the way with singing, shouting, and exploring every rock and flower. Russ and Lois followed behind, hand in hand, quite content after three years of marriage. Mike and Michelle were next with their arms around each other, whispering secrets with little smiles, like two people who could hardly wait until that August wedding.

Then along came Mom and Dad. After twenty-four years together, they still hold hands. In fact, they even steal a little smooch when no one's looking. They aren't rich or famous or powerful. They are just a man and a woman walking along a dirt road with their children—and, by God's grace, some of the most blessed people on the face of the earth.

Now if our responsibility is to put in a little extra work, a little more study, a little more prayer, a little more patience, a little more forgiveness, and a whole lot of gratitude in order to be that good dad and mom, it's worth it.

We can guarantee, it's worth it.

Topical Index